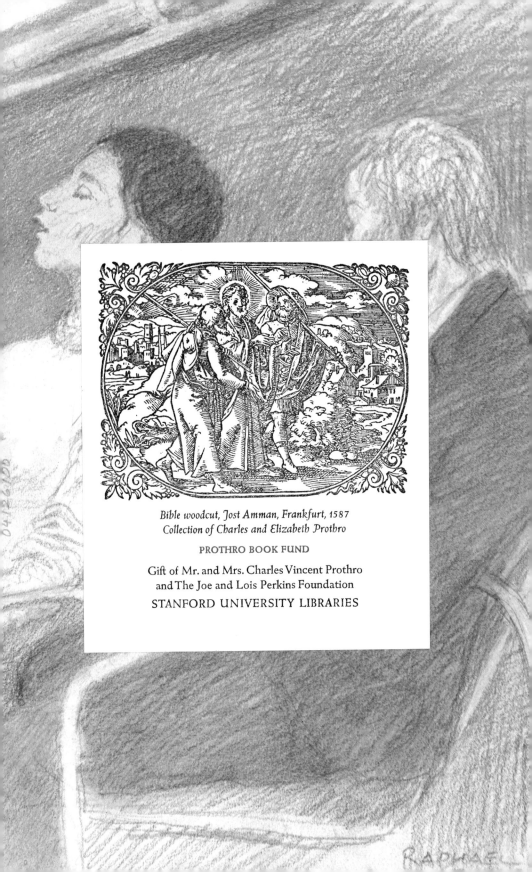

Lost in America

RAPHAEL
SOYER

Lost in America

Isaac Bashevis Singer

Paintings and Drawings by
Raphael Soyer

1981

Doubleday & Company, Inc., Garden City, New York

Library of Congress Cataloging in Publication Data

Singer, Isaac Bashevis, 1904–
Lost in America.

Autobiographical.
1. Singer, Isaac Bashevis, 1904–   —Biography.
2. Authors, Yiddish—Biography.   I. Soyer, Raphael,
1899–   II. Title.
PJ5129.S49Z465   839'.0933   [B]
ISBN: 0-385-15756-8
Library of Congress Catalog Card Number: 79–6037

LIST OF ILLUSTRATIONS

Drawings

Frontispiece (*p. iv*)

This work as well as the two volumes which preceded it, *A Little Boy in Search of God* and *A Young Man in Search of Love,* does not pretend to be completely autobiographical. Because many of the people described in them are still alive, and for other reasons, I could not tell the story of my life in the usual style of a memoir. Actually, I don't believe that the story of any human life can be written. It is beyond the power of literature. I had to skip events that I consider important. I had to distort facts as well as dates and places of occurrences in order not to hurt those who were close to me. I consider this work no more than fiction set against a background of truth. I would call the whole work: contributions to an autobiography I never intend to write.

The book was translated from the Yiddish by my nephew, Joseph Singer. I am delighted to have my friend the great artist Raphael Soyer illustrate the work. My thanks to them and to my devoted editor, Eve Roshevsky.

I.B.S.

Lost in America

CHAPTER ONE

I

At the onset of the 1930s, my disillusionment with myself reached a stage in which I had lost all hope. If truth be told, I had had little of it to lose. Hitler was on the verge of assuming power in Germany. The Polish fascists proclaimed that as far as the Jews were concerned they had the same plans for them as did the Nazis. Gina had died and only then did I realize what a treasure of love, devotion, faith in God and in human values I had lost. Stefa had married the rich Mr. Leon Treitler. My brother Joshua, his wife, Genia, and their younger son, Yosele, had gone to America, where he would work for *The Jewish Daily Forward*. Their elder son, Yasha, a lad of fourteen, had died of pneumonia. The boy's death drove me into a depression that remains with me to this day. It was my first direct contact with death.

My father also died around this time. Even though over forty years have passed, I still cannot go into details about this loss. All I can say is that he lived like a saint and he died like one, blessed with a faith in God, His mercy, His Providence. My lack of this faith is actually the story which I am about to tell.

The status of Yiddish and Yiddish literature was such that there was no way it could worsen. Kleckin Publishing, with which I had been connected, had gone bankrupt, ceased operations. The evening newspaper *Radio* no longer required my services. The same colleagues who only a year or two before had chided me for working for a bourgeois newspaper, the so-called yellow press, thus helping to feed opiates to the masses, were now trying to peddle their own *kitsch* at half or quarter price. The disappointment with communism had imbued a good many radicals with Zionist doctrines. My only source of income now was a Yiddish newspaper in Paris which also was on the verge of suspending publication. The checks from Paris kept arriving later and later. Not only couldn't I keep two separate rooms for my two girl friends, but maintaining even one became harder from month to month.

I owed Mrs. Alpert several hundred zlotys rent, but she assured me each month that she had complete trust in me. I noticed that Marila, the maid, brought me more rolls for breakfast than she had in the past. She apparently suspected that breakfast was my only meal of the day.

I corresponded with my brother in New York, but I never complained about my lot. Although my plans depended on my brother sending me an affidavit to come to America on a tourist visa and later helping me to remain there, I seldom answered his letters. Writing letters had always been a burden for me and I envied those who found the time and the inspiration for extensive correspondence.

Others bewailed their lot to me, but I never told them about my troubles. Some writers had become experts at requesting and obtaining various grants and subsidies, but I asked nothing of anyone. Gina, may she rest in peace, had nicknamed me "the Starving Squire."

I had often seen men chasing after women, pleading for love, a kiss, an endearment. Young and even elderly writers weren't ashamed to besiege editorial offices imploring that they review their work. They praised themselves and toadied up to the editors and critics. I never could hold out a hand for love, money, or recognition. Everything had to come to me of its own or not come at all.

I denied the existence of Providence, yet I awaited its dictates. I had inherited this kind of fatalism (if not faith) from both my parents. My one consolation was that if worst came to worst, I could commit suicide.

The literary scene in Warsaw, which was so rife with favoritism, clannishness, with "you scratch my back and I'll scratch yours," with sucking up to political factions and party leaders and seeking their patronage, found in me an alien element. Even though I felt that a man cannot go through life directly but must muddle through, sneak by, smuggle himself through it, I made my accounting with the divine or Satanic forces, not with the human.

I had drifted apart from Sabina, who had broken with Stalinism and turned Trotskyite. Her brother, Mottel Duck, had done the same. Brother and sister both hoped that mankind would shortly realize that the true Messiah wasn't Stalin but Trotsky, and that the social revolution in Poland would be led by Isaac Deutscher, not by that obdurate Stalinist Isaac Gordin (who subsequently spent eleven years in one of Stalin's concentration camps).

As for me, since I didn't possess the courage to kill myself, my only chance to survive was to escape from Poland. One didn't have to be particularly prescient to foresee the hell that was coming. Only those who were totally hypnotized by silly slogans could not see what was descending upon us. There was no lack of demagogues and plain fools who promised the Jewish masses that they would fight alongside the Polish gentiles on the barricades and that, following the victory over fascism, the Jews and gentiles in Poland would evolve into brothers forever after. The pious Jewish leaders, from their side, promised that if the Jews studied the Torah and sent their children to Cheders and yeshivas, the Almighty would perform miracles in their behalf.

I had always believed in God, but I knew enough of Jewish history to doubt in His miracles. In Chmielnitzki's times, Jews had studied the Torah and given themselves up to Jewishness perhaps more than in all the generations before and after. There was no Enlightenment or heresy at that time. The tortured and massacred victims were all God-fearing Jews. I had written a book about that period, *Satan in Goray*. It hadn't yet appeared in book form but it had been published in the magazine *Globus*. I hadn't received a penny in payment. Quite the contrary, I had to contribute toward the cost of the printing and paper.

A person filled with my kind of doubt is by nature lonely. I had only two friends among the Yiddish writers: Aaron Zeitlin and J. J. Trunk.

Aaron Zeitlin was some six or seven years older than I. I considered him one of the greatest poets in world literature. He was a master of both Yiddish and Hebrew, but his enormous creative force was better demonstrated in his Yiddish writings. He was a man of great knowledge, a spiritual giant among spiritual dwarfs. When the Yiddish PEN Club in Warsaw issued my book *Satan in Goray* prior to my departure for America, Zeitlin wrote the Introduction for it. The printed book, with its Introduction, didn't reach me until I was already in America.

We were both lonely men. We both knew that a holocaust was descending upon us. I often visited Zeitlin in his apartment on Sienna Street. We even tried collaborating on a book about the mad philosopher Otto Weininger. Sometimes Zeitlin visited me in the furnished rooms I kept changing. He supported himself by writing articles for the newspaper *The Express*, which occasionally published my little stories.

Intellectually and literarily, we were as close as two writers can be, but we were totally different in character. Zeitlin's number-one passion was literature, especially religious literature and everything pertaining to it. My number-one passion was the adventures of love, the endless variations and tensions peculiar to the relations between the sexes.

Zeitlin was well versed in Russian, Polish, Hebrew, French, and German literature, all of which he read in the original. He discovered writers and thinkers who had been forgotten with time or had never been recognized. For all his erudition, his poetry remained original. He mimicked no one, since he himself was often greater than those he studied. He was a faithful husband to his pretty but cold wife, whom he had married in an arranged match. He dedicated some of his poems to her. He was immensely grateful that a half-assimilated Warsaw girl, the daughter of a wealthy man, had agreed to wed him instead of some doctor or lawyer more suited to her personality. Oddly, she had a job in the burial division of the Jewish Communal Organization and she didn't give up this somber post after the wedding or even after she had given birth to a son, Risia. She spoke Polish to the child, not the language in which her husband wrote. I rarely saw the couple together.

There was an unwritten law among the wives of Yiddish writers and of the great number of so-called Yiddishists that their children should be raised to speak the Polish language. My brother's wife was no exception. The husbands had to accede. Only Chasidim and the poor, especially in the small towns, spoke Yiddish to their children.

My other friend, who was also Zeitlin's friend, J. J.

Trunk, was some twenty years older than I, the son of a rich man, an owner of buildings in the city of Lodz, and the grandson of a famous rabbi whom Trunk's nouveau riche great-grandfather had arranged to marry his daughter.

These two forebears, the merchant and the rabbi, waged a war within Trunk the man and Trunk the writer. Trunk had a good eye for people and situations. He also had a sense of humor. In later years he wrote a ten-volume set of memoirs, which are of great value as a document of Jewish life in Poland. He loved literature and he was virtually desperate to make a mark as a writer. But his writing lacked something that prevented him from achieving this. We, his friends, knew it. Chekhov once said about some Russian writer that he lacked those doubts that give talent gray hair. Trunk was and remained an amateur, albeit a gifted one. He was too cheerful, too gullible about all kinds of "isms," too naïve to be a true artist. For the very reason that he came from a rich home he resolved to become a socialist. Yet even his socialism somehow didn't agree with his character and he had constantly to justify himself to both his party comrades and to us, Zeitlin and me.

Trunk's wife, Dacha, shared his heritage of wealth and manner. Generations of Polish Jews spoke from the couple's lips. Their every word, every tone and gesture exemplified Polish-Jewish life-style, a Polish-Jewish naïvete. The husband and wife were as close as a brother and sister, and as distant as a brother and sister can sometimes be. He was fair, blue-eyed, stout. A boyish joy exuded from his eyes along with a youthful mischievousness. Dacha was lean, dark, and her black eyes reflected the vexation of the put-upon wife. Her only consolation in life was books. The Trunks had one daughter—a tall, slim, blond girl resembling the Polish aristocratic debutantes who rode horseback along Ujazdowe Allee and in Lazienki Park. It is perhaps no coincidence that during the Second World War this proud maiden converted and became a devoted Catholic. Her husband, a Christian, died during the Polish uprising in 1945.

Yes, Zeitlin, Trunk, and I were close friends. We published our works in the same magazines and anthologies of which I, the youngest, was occasionally a co-editor. I often visited their homes. But as pressing as my need was, it never occurred to me to ask them for a loan. I had already become a member of the Yiddish Writers' Club and even of the PEN Club, but I remained boyishly bashful and I never took any of my girl friends there. (Zeitlin never asked me about my private affairs. I did occasionally boast to Trunk of my alleged conquests.) The Trunks were both much older than I, and they considered me a half-crazy prodigy who was here one minute and vanished the next, like one of the demons or sprites I described in my stories. My brother also had given up trying to put my life into some kind of order. After he went to America, I became a riddle even to myself. I did things of which I was ashamed. I waged love affairs on several fronts. They all began casually and they all quickly turned serious and led me into countless deceptions and complications. I stole love, but I was always caught in the act, entangled in my lies, and I had constantly to defend myself, make holy promises, and take vows I couldn't keep. My victims castigated me with the foulest names, but my betrayals apparently didn't repel them sufficiently to get rid of me.

2

It was summer again and the heat engulfed Warsaw. Again I managed to have two residences—this time, one in Warsaw and one in the country, between Swider and Otwock. I still wrote for that Parisian Yiddish newspaper that was about to close, and from time to time I published a fragment of a story in *The Express*.

I had moved out of Mrs. Alpert's, but I had promised her and Marila to return at the first opportunity if the room was still available. At the same time I knew that I would never go back since at that time I had already obtained an affidavit to America from my brother and I was waiting for a tourist visa from the American consul. I had also applied for a foreign passport but it turned out that I lacked the required documents. I had a premonition that I would never leave Poland and that all my endeavors were for naught.

The days were long in the summer. It wasn't until ten

o'clock that the last remnants of sunset vanished from sight. By three in the morning, the birds already commenced to twitter in my caricature of a dacha. My girl friend Lena and I both slept in the nude since our garret room was baked by the sun all day, roasting our bodies like an oven. It wasn't until dawn that some cool breezes from the pine forests began to blow. The entire villa was one enormous ruin. The roof had holes, and when it rained we had to set up buckets to catch the water. The floor was rotted and infested with vermin. The mice had fled for lack of food. For the sum of one hundred and fifty zlotys, we had rented a room for the whole season. Actually, we had the entire house to ourselves, since no one else would move into this building. The doors to all the rooms stood open. The mattresses on the beds were torn, with rusted springs protruding. Occasionally, when the wind blew, the whole house shook as swarms of demons whistled and howled.

Lena and I had grown accustomed to the evil powers. They scampered over the stairs at night, opened and slammed doors, moved furniture. Even though Lena considered herself a hundred percent atheist and mocked me and my writings about the supernatural, she confessed that she had glimpsed phantoms in the corridors. At every opportunity Lena quoted Marx, Lenin, Trotsky, and Bukharin, yet she was afraid to go to the outhouse at night and she used a chamber pot. The reason she gave was that the outhouse was overgrown with weeds and

snakes lurked there. We were given a kerosene lamp by the owner, but we seldom lit it, since the moment a light came on, moths, gnats, and other insects entered through the broken windowpanes. Huge beetles emerged from holes and cracks in the floor. I covered the vat of water I brought in each day from the pump, else dozens of drowned creatures would be found floating there in the morning.

I had inherited Lena from Sabina. They were close friends for a time. They had even spent several months together in Pawiak Prison, in the women's section nick-named "Serbia." There, in their prison cell, they had fallen out because Sabina had become a Trotskyite while Lena continued to swear allegiance to Comrade Stalin. Lena had been released on bail and was supposed to stand trial, which had been scheduled months before, but she had jumped bail because new witnesses had been found for the prosecution and she would surely have been sentenced to many years imprisonment.

She had come to me in Warsaw requesting a night's sanctuary because she was, as she said, surrounded by police spies. I had only one narrow iron bed in my furnished room and she slept with me not just that one night, but for more than two weeks. She called me a capitalistic lackey even as she clamped her lips onto mine. She complained that my mystical stories helped to perpetuate fascism, but she tried to translate some of them into Polish. She swore to me that she had undergone a gynecological operation that had rendered her sterile, but she was already in her fifth month that summer. She said that she wanted to have a child by me even if the world were destroyed the next day. She assured me that the ultimate struggle between justice and exploitation was coming and, if truth triumphed, she wouldn't need my support. I could go to America if I wanted to escape the unavoidable day of revenge by the Polish masses. The revolution would reach there as well.

It was empty talk. Actually, she wandered through the ruin I had rented like a caged beast. She didn't have a penny and was in danger of being arrested. Lena came from a Chasidic household. Her father, Solomon Simon Yabloner, was a follower of the Gora Rabbi. He had driven his daughter from the house when she got involved with the Communists. He observed a period of mourning over her, as did her mother, three brothers, and two sisters. Solomon Simon was known as a strong-willed fanatic. When his children did something that displeased him, he struck them, even after they were married. In the Gora study house at 22 Franciszkanska Street, it was said that Solomon Simon had defied even the Rabbi himself. Lena (her true name was Leah Freida) told me that she would sooner hang herself than go back home to her reactionary clan. She was tall for a girl, dark as a gypsy, flat-chested as a man. Her hair was cut short. A cigarette always dangled between her full lips. She didn't trim or tweeze her thick eyebrows. Her pitch-black eyes exuded a masculine resoluteness and the frustration of one who, due to some biological error, has been born into the wrong gender. She was anything but my type. She had confessed lesbian tendencies to me. For me to associate with such a woman, and to become father of her child, was an act of madness. But I had already accustomed myself to my queer behavior. For some reason unknown to myself, this wild woman evoked within me an exaggerated sense of compassion. Although she said at every opportunity that I need assume no responsibility for her and that I was free to do as my heart desired, she clung to me. She was a coil of contradictions. One day she swore eternal love to me. The next day she said that she wanted to become pregnant because the court would be inclined to be more lenient with a mother. Now that she was a Trotskyite, she hadn't the slightest urge to do time for having served Stalin.

Our room had a wooden balcony that was rotted and sagging from years of rain and snow. Each time I stepped out onto it I had the feeling it was about to collapse under me. From there I could see the railroad tracks and the pine woods as well as the sanatoriums where thousands of consumptives slowly gasped out their lungs.

That summer only a few of my sketches were printed in *The Express* and the checks from Paris were delayed for so long that I had lost count of how much was coming to me. Years ago Lena had learned the trade of corsetmaking but for that you needed a special sewing machine, fishbone, scissors, and other paraphernalia.

Our possessions in our refuge consisted of a pot, a pan, some tin cutlery, and several books. The handyman of the villa, a Russian named Demienty, was a drunk. He supplied us with the buckets with which to catch the water when it rained. His wife had left him for another Russian. The landlord had stopped paying him wages. When Demienty wasn't lying drunk, he roamed through the woods with a rifle shooting hares, rabbits, birds. Someone had told Lena that Demienty ate cats and dogs. The villa was due to be demolished soon and used as a site for a sanatorium.

Lena and I both lived for the present. In order to get through the day—and sometimes the miserable nights as well—I fantasized that I was already dead, one of those legendary corpses which, instead of resting in the cemetery, leave their graves to reside in the world of chaos. I had described such living dead in my stories and now in my imagination I had become one of my own protagonists. Since I was a corpse, I told myself, what need had I to worry? What could happen to me? A corpse could even afford to sin.

As I stood on the balcony that night I figured out my plans for the day. I had no real reason for going to Warsaw and spending the few zlotys for the fare, but I had to see the few people with whom I was still connected in this worst of all worlds. No one in Warsaw knew my

Swider address. I had no telephone. I never saw a letter carrier enter this has-been villa. Perhaps the check from Paris had come? Maybe there was an answer from the American consul? Maybe there was a letter from Joshua waiting? It was too early to dress and I went back to bed. Lena was awake too. She was sitting on the edge of the bed smoking a cigarette. For an instant I could see her naked body in the glow of its tip. She asked, "What time are you dashing to Warsaw?"

"Ten o'clock."

"So early? Well, it's all the same. Bring me back something to read, at least. Yesterday I finished Dreiser's *An American Tragedy*."

"Is it good?"

"Neither good, nor bad. There is nothing American about this tragedy."

"I'll drop by Bresler's and bring you a whole stack of books."

"Don't get lost in Warsaw."

I was hungry after last night's meager supper. I was in a mood for fresh rolls, coffee with cream, and a piece of herring, but all we had was stale bread and a package of chicory. The little bit of milk that remained had turned sour overnight. Maybe it's already time to return to the grave? I asked myself. But somehow, I wasn't ready yet. Experience had taught me that whenever things grow extremely bad and I think that the end is near, something inevitably happens that seems a miracle. Though I had

refuted God I still believed that somewhere in the celestial register accounts were being kept of every person, every worm, every microbe. I did not expect to fall asleep, but I did when I lay down on my torn mattress, and when I opened my eyes the sun was shining.

Lena lit the Primus stove and it began to seethe and stink of alcohol. She boiled water with chicory and handed me a thick slice of black bread smeared with jam. It seemed to me that she took a thinner slice for herself and less jam. Even though she preached equality of the sexes, a trace of respect for the male inherited from generations of grandmothers and great-grandmothers still reposed somewhere within her. I chewed the stale bread for so long that it began to taste fresh. Even the chicory and water acquired flavor when you drank it slowly. Millions of people in India, China, and Manchuria didn't even have this. Only ten years or so earlier, millions of peasants had starved to death in Soviet Russia.

There was no point in getting dressed, since the sun had already begun to bake the roof overhead. I had a clean shirt for my trip to the city, but I didn't want to get it sweaty. A few weeks before I had started a novel for which I nursed great hopes. Joshua had written that the *Forward* would publish my work if they liked it. Besides, I might be able to sell it to a Warsaw newspaper. But the longer I worked on it, the clearer it became to me that it had lost both its action and form. I tried to describe an ex-yeshiva student who had become a profes-

sor of mathematics and later grew senile, became an occultist and a believer in the mystical power of numbers,
but I lacked the experience for this type of work. Lena
had told me this right from the start.

I had failed in every area. I had actually sabotaged
myself and my own goals. I had squandered a lot of energy on this manuscript. Certain chapters had come easily to me—those in which I described the confusion and
loss of memory inherent in old age. I often had the eerie
feeling that I had been born old and senile. But I knew
too little about mathematics and nothing at all about life
at a university.

It was too early to go to the station, but I could not
spend all morning inside that ruin. Lena accompanied
me. I warned her that she might be recognized and
arrested and she contended that it would be better for
her to be imprisoned. At least she wouldn't have to worry
about a maternity clinic and a place to live after the summer was over. We strolled along in the sand, each preoc-
cupied with his own thoughts.

Lena began to speak to me and to herself:

"In what way is this miserable place better than a
prison? At the Pawiak I had a clean bed. I ate better too.
Before I had the fight with the girls, I also had more
company. Here, hours go by that you don't speak a word
to me. I warned you to put aside that ridiculous novel
but you clung to it like a drowning man to a straw. Simply watching you struggle over this damn manuscript is

more painful to me than the toughest jail. At times I feel like stopping a policeman and saying, 'Here I am.' At least, I'd find a place for my son."

"How do you know it'll be a son? It could be a daughter."

"For my part, it could be an incubus."

I tried to comfort her by saying that I would take her along to America, but she replied:

"Do me no favors. You can take your America and stick it!"

Finally, the train came and I climbed aboard. Lena turned around to go back. I had to keep reminding myself that I was a corpse, freed of all human anxieties. I was dead, dead, dead! I didn't dare forget this for even a moment.

After a lengthy wait, the train started off toward Warsaw. The car was empty. Fresh breezes blew in from the resort towns. Some vacationers already lay on folding chairs, sunbathing. In Falenica I saw a Jew standing beside a tree in a prayer shawl and phylacteries, swaying over the eighteen benedictions. He beat his breast as he intoned, "We have sinned . . . We have transgressed." At a long table sat yeshiva students while the master lectured, gesticulating and pulling at his yellow beard.

If no check came for me from Paris today, I was through for good. The only way out would be to jump into the Vistula. I received my mail not at my room on Nowolipki Street, but at the home of Leon Treitler, the husband of the former Miss Stefa and the present Madam Treitler.

I was actually going to her. All my mail came at her address. I could have called her long-distance but this was not less expensive than a third-class ticket. I had reached such a stage of isolation where Stefa and a poor cousin of mine, Esther, had become my only contact with Warsaw. Zeitlin and his wife had gone to the Zakopane Mountains for their vacation. J. J. Trunk went to some spa abroad. The Yiddish Writers' Club was deserted in the summer months.

3

Leon Treitler lived in his own building on Niecala Street, a few steps from the Saxony Gardens. The apartment consisted of eight rooms. Leon Treitler had read my stories in Yiddish and Stefa had tried translating them into Polish. She knew more Yiddish than she admitted. She no longer called it slang; she had ceased believing in assimilation. The Jews could neither become totally Polish nor would the Poles tolerate this weird minority. Stefa had been insulted several times in Polish cafes when she had gone there with her husband; she had been advised to go back to Nalewki Street or to Palestine. The anti-Semitic writers in the Polish press even attacked the converts. Some of these writers had accepted the racial theories of Hitler and Rosenberg—this at a time when the Nazi press was describing the Poles as an inferior race and maintaining that a number of their best families, such as the Majewskis and the Wolowskis, were descendants of the followers of the false messiah Jacob Frank, an Oriental Jew and a charlatan. There was even conjecture that the Polish national poet, Adam Mickie-wicz, was of that breed since on his mother's side he was a Majewski, which was the name assumed by all the Frankists who converted during the month of May. The Wolowskis, on the other hand, were the offspring of Elisha Shor, one of Frank's most learned disciples.

Warsaw lay in the grip of a heat wave. I couldn't wait until I got to Stefa's to learn whether a letter had come for me and I called her. Telephone service had already made direct dialing possible. I heard the ringing and, presently, Stefa's voice. Stefa had so utterly rejected the idea of assimilation that she often insisted on being addressed as Sheba Leah, and she called me Yitzchok, Itche, and sometimes even Itchele. She now exclaimed:

"Yitzchok, if you called me a minute before, no one would have answered! I went down to buy a paper."

"What's the news?"

"Bad as always. But I have some good news for you. There is mail for you."

"From where?"

"From halfway around the world—from Paris, from New York, from the American consul. It seems there are two letters from New York. Shall I take a look?"

"We'll look together."

"Where are you?"

"At the station."

"Come over. I'll make breakfast for you."

"I've already had my breakfast."

"Either you eat with me or I'll throw all your letters out the window."

"Sheba Leah, you're terrible!"

"That's what I am."

I had intended to walk to Niecala Street from the station to save the fare, but I now raced to catch a streetcar. What a few words can do to a corpse, I said to myself. I had come as close to Treitler's house as the streetcar would take me and I ran the few remaining steps. The janitor knew me. Even his dog didn't bark at me as he once had. On the contrary, he began to wag his tail when I entered the gate. Each time I paid a visit to this house I marveled at what time and human emotions could accomplish. I could never forget my first meeting with Stefa; how she had questioned me as I stood on the other side of the door; the contempt with which she had spoken of Yiddish and of Yiddishkeit; of how close she herself had been to suicide at that time. Now, Stefa was a rich matron and my Polish translator. A fragment of my novel had been published in a Polish newspaper and, thanks to me, her name had appeared in print for the first time. She had signed herself Stefa Janovska Treitler. Leon Treitler was so proud of seeing his name in print that he arranged an evening in honor of the occasion. Among those invited were Stefa's former friends from the *Gymnasium* and the university, several of her relatives, and Leon Treitler's partners with their wives and daughters. Champagne was drunk and speeches were made. Leon Treitler had bought a hundred copies of the paper and had had one of them framed. I had never before encountered such exaggerated respect for the printed word.

Stefa's former teacher, who was also present, made a toast and recalled that when Stefa had still been in the sixth grade at the *Gymnasium* he had predicted a literary career for her. He now prophesied that Stefa would forge a bond between Polish and Yiddish literature. The fact was that he had mistaken me for my brother. Joshua's novel had come out in Polish after he had immigrated to America and it had received favorable reviews. Oddly, the most virulent Polish anti-Semite, the infamous Nowaczynski, had written a glowing review of this book, *Yoshe Kalb.* According to his article, my brother had demonstrated the extraordinary extent of Jewish energy in his novel, and how skilled the Jew was at hypnotizing himself and others—also, how the Pole, who was by nature soft, naïve, and weak in character, could easily be influenced by the Jew and dominated by him if he didn't resist.

The prophesies made by Stefa's teacher that evening at the Treitlers' didn't come true. Outside of that single piece, no other work of mine was ever published in Polish. But a love awoke between Stefa and me that she didn't bother to conceal from her husband. We kissed in Leon Treitler's presence. He was one of those men who actually cannot exist without a *hausfreund*. He often called to reproach me for neglecting Stefa.

Leon Treitler was tiny, with a pointed skull lacking even a single hair. He had a long nose, a sharp, receding chin, a pointed Adam's apple, and jutting ears. He couldn't have weighed over a hundred pounds. He dressed like a dandy, loud ties with pearl stickpins, buckled shoes, and hats with a little brush or feather. He had a thin nasal voice and he spoke in ironical paradoxes. He always began the conversation somewhere in the middle —needling and flattering at the same time. He would say, "And even when you're a famous writer already, must you ignore every ordinary person just because he or she isn't versed in all works of Nietzsche and can't remember all of Pushkin by heart? I search for you like with candles and you hide out just as if I were your worst enemy. And even if I am an ignoramus and it's beneath your dignity to associate with one of my kind, how is it Stefa's fault? She simply dies of longing for you and you punish her for the fact that instead of marrying a poet she took a moneybags while her true love, that swindler Mark, deserted her with all his diplomas and medals."

This was Leon Treitler's style. He nipped and he

stroked. One eye winked and the other laughed. Stefa said that he was both a sadist and a masochist. He was crooked in business and was forever tied up in litigation, but he also gave money to worthy causes. Stefa swore to me that just four weeks after their wedding he had begun seeking a lover for her. He had a female secretary who knew all his tricks and who had been his lover for over twenty-five years.

Leon Treitler was different from other people in many ways. He never slept more than four hours out of the twenty-four. For breakfast, he had bread and wine; for supper, cold meat and black coffee. His sexual gratification consisted of pinching Stefa's bottom and calling her "whore." He owned a whole library of pornographic pictures.

Stefa said to me once, "What Leon Treitler really is, I'll never know if I live to be a thousand. At times I suspect that he is one of your demons."

I rang and Stefa answered. The maid had gone out to market. Stefa had gained some weight but her figure was still slim and girlish. In protest against being constantly complimented on her gentile appearance, she had dyed her hair brunette, and she wore a Star of David around her neck.

Right there in the corridor we embraced and kissed a long time. Even though she maligned Leon Treitler at every opportunity, I had long since observed that she had acquired some of his mannerisms. She pledged me her love yet at the same time she needled me. Now she took me by the ear, led me into the dining room, and said, "You'll eat with me even if you'll stand on your head!"

"Where are the letters?"

"There are no letters. I fooled you. I don't want you to go off to America and abandon me."

"Come with me."

"First eat! You're as pale as death. They wouldn't allow a skeleton into America."

I had assumed that I was full. My abdomen was bloated and I felt something akin to revulsion toward food. But the moment I bit into the first roll, I became hungry. I said, "Do me a favor and give me the letters. I swear I'll finish everything."

"Your suit is covered with hair. Wait, I'll brush you off."

She carefully plucked a hair from my lapel and examined it against the light of the sun. "A red hair?" she asked. "You told me she was a brunette."

"It's my hair."

"What? You have no hair. It's not your shade either."

"Sheba Leah, don't be silly."

"You're getting to be more like Mark every day. All you need is to forge a signature. What is it with me? It seems I attract this kind of man. One lunatic worse than the next."

"Stefa, enough!"

"You look like death warmed over and you run around

with God knows how many sluts. Once and for all I'll give up all hopes of love. This seems to be my fate and that's how it must remain. You're leaving me anyhow. I see everything clearly—you'll go off to America and I'll never hear from you again. And even if I do get a letter, it'll be all lies. Who is the redhead? Red hair doesn't simply float through Otwock and just happen to light on your lapel. Unless your former wench—what was her name—Gina—rose from her grave and paid you a visit."

"Stefa, what's wrong with you?"

"I can endure the worst betrayals, but I can't stand to be deceived. I told you as soon as we got together— everything yes, but no lies! You swore on your parents' lives—your father was still living. Is this true or not?"

"Yes, it's true."

"Who is she? What is she? Where did you meet her? Tell me the truth or I'll never look at your face again!"

"She's my cousin."

"A new lie! You never told me about any cousins. And what about this cousin? Are you having an affair with her?"

"I swear that what I am about to tell you now is the sacred truth."

"What is the truth? Speak!"

I started to tell Stefa about my cousin Esther, who was six years younger than I. When I came to Bilgoray in 1917, I was past thirteen and she was a child of eight. There evolved between us one of those silent loves that neither participant verbalizes nor even dares to think about. When I left Bilgoray for the last time in 1923, Esther was a girl of thirteen but I was a young man of nineteen teaching an evening course in Hebrew. I had begun to write, too, and was having a platonic affair with a girl. I didn't even recall shaking Esther's hand when I left the first time. A rabbi's son didn't shake hands with a girl when the family was present.

Years passed and I didn't hear from Esther. She wrote me only once, when her father, my uncle, died. Suddenly, she showed up in Warsaw, by now a grown woman of twenty-three. She had learned the milliner's trade. She had read many books in Polish and Yiddish, my stories as well. She had become "enlightened" and had given up religion. She had come to Warsaw seeking a job in her trade, but also with the intention of revealing to me what she had kept concealed for so many years. She had confided the truth to only one girl friend, Tsipele. Tsipele now lived in Warsaw too, and worked as a cashier in her uncle's stores. Esther and Tsipele shared a furnished room on Swietojerska Street, across from Krasinski's Gardens.

I presumed that Stefa would interrupt me and call me a liar, as she so often did, but she heard me out and said, "This sounds like a fairy tale out of a storybook, but it seems to be true. What did you do with this Esther? Did you manage to seduce her yet?"

"Absolutely not."

"What is her hair doing on your lapel?"

"Truly, I don't know."

"You know, you know! Wait, I'll get you your letters."

Stefa went out, then came back with a stack of letters that she flung on the table. I started to open them one after the other. My hands were trembling. One letter was from my brother. I could hardly believe my eyes. It contained a check from the *Forward* in the amount of ninety dollars. I had sent my brother one of my stories and he had sold it to the newspaper, of which he was a staff member.

I opened a second letter from America. A known American writer and critic had read my novella *Satan in Goray* and his whole letter was a paean to this work.

The American consulate demanded one additional document that would be required for the granting of a tourist visa.

The literary magazine for which I both published and served as a proofreader for a time had forwarded a letter from a reader who castigated me for writing too much about sex, saying it was not in the tradition of Yiddish literature.

My brother informed me that as soon as I obtained my foreign passport he would send me the money for the fare.

I had momentarily mislaid the letter from Paris and I searched for it among the others. Soon I discovered that I had inadvertently stuck it into my breast pocket and I now opened it. Inside lay the check for which I had been waiting so long. It was for an amount in excess of a hundred dollars.

I grew frightened by the plethora of good fortune all at one time. "You haven't earned it," someone within me exclaimed. Stefa stood there and looked at me sidelong. She asked, "What are you doing—praying?"

"Sheba Leah, you've brought me luck."

"Luck and I are not a pair."

4

Stefa accompanied me to the office of the Hebrew Immigrant Aid Society where they cashed my checks for American currency. The cashier opened a huge safe crammed from top to bottom with dollar bills. Afterward, we went to a bank where my check from Paris was cashed for nearly a thousand zlotys. I had exchanged my elegant and comfortable room at Mrs. Alpert's for a tiny cubicle on Nowolipki Street rented to me for thirty zlotys a month by a member (or a guest) of the Writers' Club, a principal of a Hebrew school and author of a grammar textbook. He and his family were away now on vacation and I actually had the entire apartment to myself, but he, M. G. Haggai, came back to Warsaw each week for a day or two and I could never know when he would show up.

It was certainly risky to bring Stefa to such a place,

but the danger at her home was even greater. Although Leon Treitler pretended that he didn't even know the meaning of jealousy, one could never forsee how he would react if he caught us together.

Stefa wouldn't go to a hotel. Her mother had died, but her father, Isidore Janovsky, was still living and he had a room in a hotel on Milna Street, nearby. He liked to roam through the streets, to chat with other old people in Krasinski's Gardens, in the Saxony Gardens, or on a bench on Iron Gate Square. Even as Stefa walked with me she kept looking behind. She told me that if her father found out about her behavior, he would have a heart attack. She also had hordes of relatives in Warsaw who envied her good fortune, and who would have loved the chance to malign her. Stefa took my arm, then quickly dropped it. Each time she walked with me in the street she had some pretext ready in case we encountered her husband, her father, or someone from her or her husband's family.

We walked into the gate of the house of Mr. Haggai's apartment and climbed the two flights of stairs. Doors stood open. Children cried, laughed, screamed. This was a respectable family building, not one for illicit loves. Before leaving Stefa's house, I had telephoned here to make sure M. G. Haggai wasn't at home. But what guarantee did I have that he hadn't come in in the interval? For renting me the room so cheaply, M. G. Haggai had stipulated that I behave decently. Tenants of the building enrolled their children in his school and I shouldn't dare do anything to damage his reputation.

I now rang the doorbell, but no one came. M. G. Haggai was surely lounging on a folding chair in Falenica reading the London Hebrew magazine *Haolam* and enjoying the fresh air. His apartment was decorated with pictures of Zionist leaders: Herzl, Max Nordau, Chlenov, Weizmann, Sokolov. There also hung here a portrait of the pedagogue Pestalozzi. Each time Stefa visited my little room she said the same thing: "This isn't a room but a hole."

This time I countered with: "Good enough for two mice."

"Speak for yourself."

I was in a hurry, since I still had to meet Esther. I had to stop by Bresler's Lending Library and select some books for Lena. I also intended to buy food, which was easier to obtain in Warsaw, as well as a small present for Lena. But Stefa had more than once said that she didn't equate lovemaking with speed. She had to begin with conversation and the subject was always the same: the reason she couldn't remain true to Treitler—he had always repelled her. He had won her in a moment of her deepest despair. One could truthfully say that he had bought her with money.

Stefa sat down on the only chair in my room and crossed her legs. Her knees had remained pointed although not as much as before. I had already had her many times, but I still felt a strong urge for her, since sooner or later we would have to part. She spoke and from time to time she took a drag on her cigarette.

I heard her say, "If someone had told me five years ago that I would be Mrs. Treitler and conducting an illicit affair with some jargon journalist, I would have considered him mad. Sometimes it seems to me that I'm no longer me but someone else—as if I were possessed by one of your dybbuks."

Abruptly, she began to study the walls.

"What do you see there?" I asked.

"I'm afraid there are bedbugs here."

"They sleep by day."

Stefa started to say something, but at that moment there was a sound in the corridor. That which I had feared had occurred—M. G. Haggai had come home on his weekly visit.

Stefa tensed. Her face twisted momentarily. M. G. Haggai coughed and mumbled to himself. I assumed that he would immediately open the door to my room but apparently he went into the living room. However, he was liable to peek into my room at any moment. It was a miracle that he hadn't arrived a half hour later.

Stefa put out her cigarette in a saucer to be used for an ashtray. "Let's get out of here! This very second!"

"Sheba Leah, it's not my fault."

"No, no, no! You are what you are, but I had no right to crawl into such a slime. All the evil forces have turned against me. Come, let us go!"

"Why are you so scared? We're both dressed. I've got a right to have visitors."

"How close did we come to being caught without our clothes? These Hebraists know everybody. Leon's daughter attended a Hebrew *Gymnasium*. He might have been her teacher there."

The door to my room opened and M. G. Haggai stuck his head inside. Outside, a heat wave raged, but he wore his overcoat, a derby (a "melon" as it was called in Warsaw), a high stiff collar, and a black cravat. He had a round face and a gray goatee. A pair of horn-rimmed glasses with thick lenses sat upon his broad nose. He hadn't even managed to put down the briefcase he was carrying under his arm. Seeing a woman, he recoiled, but soon after he crossed the threshold and said, "Excuse me. I didn't know you were here and that you had company besides. My name is Haggai," he said, turning to Stefa. "The name of a prophet among us Jews. But I'm no prophet. I thought that our friend here was away on vacation, not here in the hot city. I must come in every week since I am the principal and owner of a private school and this is the time when the students are being enrolled for the coming term. What is your esteemed name, if one may ask?"

Stefa didn't respond. It was as if she had completely lost possession of herself. It was I who replied. "This is Miss Anna Goldsober."

"Goldsober, eh? I know three Goldsober families in Warsaw," Haggai said. "One is Dr. Zygmunt Goldsober, a famous ophthalmologist. Someone told me he is even more distinguished than Dr. Pinnes, or is it *Professor* Pinnes? The second Goldsober family has a wholesale dry-goods business on Gesia Street. Their son attended my school. He is already a father himself. The third Goldsober is a lawyer. To which of these Goldsobers do you belong?"

"To neither—" Stefa said.

"So? You are not a Litvak?"

"A Litvak? No."

M. G. Haggai winked at me. "I have something to discuss with you. If you'll excuse us, madam, I'd like a word with him alone."

I followed him into the living room. He slowly removed his hat and coat and put down the briefcase. His eyes, through the thick lenses, appeared unnaturally big and stern. He said, "Your visitor is no Goldsober as you have misrepresented her, and she is surely no miss."

"How do you know what she is or isn't?"

"A miss doesn't wear a wedding ring. You gave me a promise and you haven't kept it. I don't want to be your mentor, but you can't receive such visitors at my house. You'll have to move out. I'm sorry. When is your month up?"

"At the end of the coming week."

"You'll have to find another room."

"I've committed no sin, but if that's what you want, I'll do as you ask."

"I'm sorry."

I went back to my room and Stefa stood there already wearing her hat and holding her bag, ready to go. She asked, "Why did you pick Goldsober of all names? Oh, that one is a pest. The whole time he kept staring at my wedding ring. What did he say to you? Probably asked you to move. If a grave would open for me, I'd jump into it this minute."

She said this in Polish, but the expression was pure Yiddish.

5

We walked in the direction of Karmelicka Street and Stefa spoke, as if to herself: "This isn't for me. Warsaw isn't Paris but a small town. My father lives but a few blocks from here. He is liable to come upon us at any moment. He claims to be half blind, but the things he shouldn't see, he sees well enough. You know what? Let's head in the opposite direction. Where does this street lead to?"

"To Karolkowa, to Mlinarska, to the Jewish cemetery."

"Come, let us go there. I don't want to disappoint my father. He feels that I've enjoyed a stroke of great fortune. It's no trifle to be Mrs. Treitler. The very title makes me nauseous. I envy my mother. She knows nothing anymore. If people knew how happy the dead are, they wouldn't struggle so hard to hold on to life. The first thing my mother did after my sister died was to use her last few zlotys and buy a plot next to hers. Now they lie side by side. People still go to visit the graves of their parents. They really believe that the dead lie there waiting to be told all the troubles that have befallen those close to them. Here is a droshky. . . . Hey!"

"Where do you want to go?" I asked.

"What's the difference? Let's go someplace. You said yourself that your cousin, or whoever she may be, won't be home until seven. Today belongs to me."

"Where do the lady and gentleman wish to go?" the cab driver asked.

Stefa hesitated for a moment. "To Niecala Street. But don't turn around. Go by way of Iron Street and from there through Chlodna, Electoralna—"

"That's the long way around."

"You'll get double your fare."

"Giddy up!"

"We should have stayed there in the first place," I said.

"You had to cash your checks. For me, nothing comes easy. But since you're going away to America, what difference does it make? To have a maid is to have a spy in the house. I had enough of my parents' maid spying on me and reporting every thing to my mother. If a young man phoned me occasionally, she ran to tell her. She herself was a widow. Her husband died four weeks after their wedding. Strange, she never spied on my

sister. Now, I've got Jadwiga on my back. She worked
for Leon years before he married me. She remembers his
first wife and she looks at me as if I had murdered her.
His daughters feel that way about me too, as do the
neighbors. I'm nothing but an intruder. What will I do
after you're gone? Start an affair with a new liar? Three
liars in a lifetime is enough for me. In the morning
when I look in the mirror, especially after a good night's
sleep, I see a young person. But when I look at myself in
the evenings, I see a broken woman ready for the scrap
pile. Mark deserted me physically and shattered me spirit-
ually—that's the truth. Going to live with Leon Treitler
was for me a catastrophe. Then my foul luck directed
me to start up with you . . . You don't forge promissory
notes, but you're made of the same stuff as he—a timid
adventurer."

"Thanks for the compliment."

The droshky entered Chlodna, passed the fire station
with its huge brass bell, the Seventh Police Precinct,
then turned into Electoralna Street, where the Hospital
of the Holy Ghost was located. Flocks of pigeons soared
over the roofs and perched on the heads, shoulders, and
arms of the holy statues. Below, some of them ate from
the hands of an old woman. Every street we passed,
every building, evoked within me memories of my childhood. The Poles still considered us aliens, but the Jews
had helped build this city and had assumed an enormous
participation in its commerce, finances, and industry.

Even the statues in this church represented images of Jews.

Just as if Stefa could read my mind, she remarked, "We Jews are damned. Why?"

"Because we love life too much."

The droshky came to Niecala Street. Stefa's maid, Jadwiga, had left a note in the kitchen saying that Mr. Treitler would be detained at his work and would have dinner with his partner at a restaurant. Stefa had told Jadwiga that she would be eating dinner out, and Jadwiga had gone to visit a friend who had given birth to an illegitimate child and had to stay with it.

Stefa said, "I'm beginning to believe that there is a God."

"Since He obliges us, then He exists."

"Don't be so sarcastic. If He is truly our father and we are His children as the Bible states, He *should* oblige us from time to time."

"He is your husband's father too."

"That which I'm doing benefits him too. He wants it subconsciously. Where are my cigarettes?"

Stefa had become momentarily cheerful. We hadn't eaten lunch and she went to the kitchen to fix us a quick bite. She put on a short apron that lent her a particularly feminine allure. I sat down at the kitchen table and reread the letters I had received that morning. I also recounted the money. I told myself that this was one of the happiest days of my life. To avoid it being ruined, I

offered up a silent prayer to the God whose commandments I was breaking. Actually, this was what thieves, murderers, and rapists did. Even Hitler mentioned the Almighty in his speeches.

6

Night had already fallen by the time I said good-bye to Stefa. My wristwatch indicated a quarter to ten. Our mutual desire and our powers had never been as strong as during those long hours. Usually, gratification is contingent upon ennui as Schopenhauer contends, but my satiety that day brought no tedium. Only the worries returned. I had committed a folly in cashing both checks. I was afraid now of being robbed or of springing a hole in my breast pocket and losing my fortune. I no longer had time to visit Bresler's Lending Library, which was closed by now anyhow. The stores were all closed too and I wouldn't even be able to buy Lena the delicacies she preferred. There was barely any time left to visit my cousin. What's more, I had promised Lena to come back early, but I wasn't sure now whether I could even catch the last train to Otwock, which left at midnight and arrived around 1 A.M.

Thank God, an empty taxi came by. I was only afraid lest the driver should—through some mysterious power —ascertain that I was carrying a sum amounting to over two hundred dollars and try to rob me. The taxi made the trip to Swietojerska Street in five minutes. I climbed the stairs, which were illuminated by a tiny gaslight. On the second floor I bumped into Esther's roommate, Tsipele. She was going out, probably in order to leave us alone. She wore a straw hat that Esther had made for her. Tsipele had once been my pupil in an evening course in Hebrew I had taught in Bilgoray. She had learned no Hebrew from me, but just the same, she still called me "moreh"—teacher.

I had never done this before, but I kissed her. Her face lay completely in shadow. She exclaimed, "Oh, Moreh, what are you doing?"

Tsipele was blond, taller than Esther, and younger by a year. Esther had told me that Tsipele's uncle, for whom she worked as an assistant bookkeeper, was in love with her. He gave her money, sent her flowers, brought her candy, and took her to the theater, the opera, and to restaurants. Tsipele's aunt was suspicious that she was trying to steal her husband away, but Esther assured me that Tsipele remained a virgin. The whole world is either crazy with love or crazy with hate, I said to myself. I knocked and Esther opened the door. Her hair was a dark red, her face densely freckled. We had both inherited our coloring from our Grandmother Hannah, the rebbetzin.

From the day of her wedding at barely twelve years of age, no one, not even Grandfather, had seen her hair, for she shaved her skull. Only her eyebrows were red. Our

grandfather, Jacob Mordecai, was a year older than she. As a child he had acquired the reputation of a prodigy. When he was nine he gave a sermon in the house of study and scholars came to debate with him on Talmudic subjects. Grandmother's father, Isaac, after whom I am named, was a merchant and a man of wealth, who had arranged for Jacob Mordecai to marry his only daughter, Hannah. Grandmother Hannah had a fiery temper and, although her husband became known as a sage and she couldn't write a Yiddish letter without errors, whenever they quarreled she called him a Litvak pig. This was undeserved, as he had been born in Miedzyrzec, which was in Poland, not in Lithuania.

Our grandparents were no longer living, but their blood flowed in our veins. When Esther spoke I could hear in her words, and even more so in her intonation, generations of scholars, pious women, as well as something that seemed non-Jewish, even typically goyish. Within our genetic cells, the subjugators and the subjugated were forced to co-exist. I had warned myself not to become involved with Esther. I was honest enough to tell her that I had no intention of getting married. I told her about Stefa and Lena as well as of my efforts to settle in America. But Esther had been influenced by the new concepts. She wasn't engaged to any man. There was no purpose in saving her virginity for someone she didn't know or who might never turn up. Her female co-workers at the millinery shop all had lovers. Most young men no longer required that their prospective wives be virgins. The situation in the world was desperate, and that of the Jews in Poland especially. So why wait?

Esther and I now lay on the bed and from time to time I glanced at my watch. I didn't dare miss my train to Otwock! I felt guilty, but I had the consolation that I wasn't deceiving Esther. We both tried to steal something which belonged to us only. Esther's face was flushed nevertheless. She told me that she would never forget me and that if she was spared she would come to me in America. I had noticed that Esther too glanced at her wristwatch. Tsipele would be returning shortly.

We said good-bye, kissed at length, and arranged a rendezvous for the coming week when I would absolutely, positively have more time for her. When we were at the door, Esther mumbled, "I hope you were careful."

"Yes, a hundred percent!"

The gaslight illuminating the stairs was out, which meant that the gate was already closed. I had descended half a flight when I heard Esther's voice. She called to me to come back. It turned out that in my excitement the roll of bills—all the money I had collected today at the bank and at the HIAS office—had fallen out of my breast pocket.

I seized it and stuck it back in my pocket. "I'm crazy, crazy as a loon!"

I started racing down the stairs in the dark. I had lost some two to three minutes. I would have to wait until the janitor opened the gate for me. I began to search for the bell with which to rouse him. I couldn't find it. I tapped around like a blind man. Luckily, someone rang the bell on the outside. The janitor was in no hurry to open up, and only after a long wait did he come out of his cubicle, grumbling, as did all janitors I have ever met. I groped in my pocket for a coin with which to tip him, but I couldn't find one. I was almost sure that I had had coins in both pockets of my jacket. I must have dropped them at Esther's. The janitor paused and stretched out a hand for my coin, and when I began to apologize, he spat and cursed. I heard him say *"Psia krew"*—dog's blood. He opened the gate with a large key and by the light of the streetlamp I saw Tsipele.

"Moreh!"

She made a move as if to embrace me, but I only managed to say "Good night!" I hadn't a moment to lose now. I ran in the direction of Nalewki Street. I had to catch either a streetcar, a droshky, or a taxi—whichever came first. One taxi passed after another—they were all heading away from the depot, not toward it. The streetcars also ran in the opposite direction. All I could do was run. It was eight minutes to twelve by the time I got to the Gdansk Station. Thank God there was no line in front of the ticket seller's cage and I quickly bought my ticket. This wasn't a local train running only between Warsaw and Otwock, but one that ran as far as Lvov. The cars were crowded with passengers, mostly Jewish salesmen and storekeepers from the provinces. Almost every one carried sacks, bundles, or crates of goods. Several coaches were full of soldiers. No civilian passengers were allowed in there. The soldiers stood by the open windows and mocked the harassed Jews racing from car to car and dragging their bundles. The second-class cars were occupied mainly by officers.

I squeezed myself into one of the third-class cars as best I could. All the seats were taken. Some passengers read Yiddish newspapers, some chewed unfinished suppers from paper bags, others leaned their heads against the walls trying to catch some sleep. All the faces reflected the fatigue of the Diaspora, the fear of tomorrow. The train was scheduled to depart at midnight, but the clock showed a quarter past twelve and we still hadn't moved. The car smelled of cigarette smoke, garlic, onions, sweat, and the latrine. Facing me stood a girl with a gold, or gold-plated, Star of David hanging around her neck. She was trying to read a novel by the Polish sex novelist Gabriela Zapolska in the murky light of the gas lamp. Same as I, she had accepted the kind of secular Jewishness that defies all definitions.

This time, the trip from Warsaw to Otwock took not an hour but only half that time. The train stopped there for just a minute and discharged a few passengers. I started off across the sandy path leading to the broken-down villa where Lena waited for me. I had brought her neither food nor travel books, but I had resolved that first

thing in the morning I would go to Slavin's Bookstore and buy her a book and take her to a restaurant.

Otwock, with all its consumptives, was asleep. Inside the sanatoriums' morgues lay those who earlier that day had breathed their last. I climbed the dark stairs of the house we lived in and every board squeaked beneath my heavy shoes. I opened the door to our room. Our bed stood empty. I called, "Lena! Lena!" and an echo answered. I opened the door to the balcony even though I could see through the glass door that no one was there. I began searching for matches, but I didn't find them. It was Lena who smoked, not I, and she had probably taken them with her. After a while my eyes had grown accustomed to the dark and I began to see by the light of the stars and that of a distant streetlight. Lena had taken her coat and her satchel. She hadn't left a note.

I went out onto the balcony and stood there for a long time contemplating the heavenly bodies. I asked them mutely, "What do you say to all this?" And I imagined that they replied, "We have seen it all before."

CHAPTER TWO

I

Everything came hard to me—the passport, the visa. Even a naïve Yankee like the American consul didn't believe that I was being invited to America to speak about literature. I looked like a frightened boy, not a lecturer. He posed many questions to me through his interpreter, a Jewish girl with a big head of bleached curly hair. The consul had received information from someone that I was having an affair with a leftist woman and he asked, "How is it you come to be involved with such individuals?"

I was overcome by a silly sense of frankness and I countered his question with another: "Where else can you get free love?"

The interpreter laughed, and after she had translated my response, laughter broke out among the other officials.

This answer, like all my others, was not true. Many of the so-called bourgeois girls were already far from being chaste. The only difference lay in that the bourgeois girls weren't interested in some Yiddish scribbler who was a pauper besides. They sought doctors, lawyers, or wealthy merchants. They demanded to be taken to the theater, to cafes. Neither was I interested in their banalities. With Lena at least I could have discussions, dash her hopes for a better world. To her I was a cynic, not a *schlemiel.*

After a long interrogation, and shaking his head dolefully, the consul affixed the stamp designating a tourist visa in my passport. He shrugged his shoulders and wished me a happy journey. Oddly, all the lies I told the consul that day came true years later. How does Spinoza put it in his *Ethics:* There are no lies, only crippled truths. I might add, The truer a truth is, the more crippled it appears to us.

Of course I felt exalted that I had been granted, one might say, the privilege of life, a reprieve from Hitler's executioners. Yet, at the same time, I thought, This is man. His life and death depend on a piece of paper, a signature, the whim of another, be he consul, *starosta,* judge, or commissar. When I left the consul's office, I passed a hallway where many others like me were waiting. Their eyes seemed to ask, Did he get his visa or was he refused it? And what will be *my* fate? On that pre-spring day I felt more than ever the dependence of man, his helplessness. I envied the cobblestones in the streets, which needed no passports, no visas, no novels, no favors. It wasn't I that was alive and they that were dead, I told myself. Quite the contrary. The stones lived and I was dead.

From time to time I fingered the passport in my breast pocket. Had all this really happened? And what had I done to deserve this? Again and again I stopped at shop windows and leafed through the passport. It was valid for a period of six months, as was the visa. After that I would have to apply for an extension at the Polish consulate in New York and to the Immigration Service in Washington. Even if it became possible to obtain a permanent visa outside of the quota, I couldn't obtain it in America. According to law, I'd have to go outside the country to apply for this visa—to Canada or Cuba, for instance. But to do that required another visa. . . .

Several years before, when I had been exempted from military service, it was Gina who had been waiting for me to hear the news. But Gina no longer lived. Lena had vanished. As for Stefa, my visa to America was hardly good news. She told me this at every opportunity. Nor would my cousin Esther be pleased that I'd be leaving.

Although M. G. Haggai had asked me to move out that summer day, I still lived there. He had changed his mind. I had convinced him that I had committed no sin in his house. He enjoyed chatting with me about literature and about the fact that most Hebrew writers didn't know their grammar. They made errors in their texts and the critics knew even less than they did. Haggai often told me that in order to know Hebrew properly one had to devote one's whole life to it, and sometimes it appeared that even one life wasn't enough.

I telephoned Stefa now. She wasn't home. Esther had

a job at a milliners with a store and workshop on Zabia Street and she wasn't due home till evening. I went to have lunch at the Writers' Club and possibly to try to telephone Stefa again. The Writers' Club wasn't yet twenty years old but I had the feeling that it had existed forever. A number of the writers had grown old; many had died; a few had grown senile. Everyone who belonged to the club had endless complaints against the world, against God, against other writers, editors, reviewers, even against the readers and their bad taste.

I had the urge to show off my visa to somebody, but I decided against it. The telephone rang and the woman at the hatcheck counter came to fetch me. It was Stefa. I told her the news and she exclaimed, "Come right over!"

I went out into the street and raced toward Niecala Street. Warsaw suddenly appeared to me a foreign city. I barely recognized the stores, the buildings, the tramways. I recalled something out of the Gemara: "That which is about to be burned is like already burned." I paraphrased it in my mind: That which one is preparing to abandon is like already abandoned.

As usual before spring, cold winds blended with warm breezes. One tree in the Saxony Gardens bloomed all by itself amidst the other bare trees and bushes. A few days before I had seen a blossom fall along with snow while a butterfly fluttered amidst it all. I wanted to leave the city, yet at the same time I already longed for this city where I hadn't properly settled but had merely sampled a meager portion of its allures. I now compared Warsaw to a book one must lay aside just as the story is approaching its climax. I rang Stefa's doorbell and she came to answer. While still in the doorway, she said, "I should congratulate you, but it's all happening faster than I can digest it."

"Why did you happen to phone to the club today?" I asked.

"Oh, my cursed intuition. Last night, Leon said, 'You'll see. Your lover will go away and not even write to you.'"

"Is that what he called me?"

"Yes, he knows everything. Sometimes he speaks of you as if he knows nothing, then suddenly he sounds as if he knows it all. Actually I wanted to ring you at Haggai's, only I made a mistake and dialed the Writers' Club instead. Come, show me the visa. We'll have to make a party, or whatever. Before you even began talking about America I knew that you would do the same as Mark—leave me. In New York someone already waits who doesn't even know of your existence. But she'll take you in her arms and you'll be hers. That's how destiny works. One thing I want to assure you, I'll never depend upon anyone again."

"Stefa, you promised to tell me the truth." I heard my lips form the words. I knew that Stefa knew what I meant. That day when she phoned me at Mrs. Alpert's and I asked if she had had a boy or a girl, she told me that she had had nothing, and her answer remained the same thereafter. I could never determine from her if she had had the child or a late abortion, or possibly had given birth to a stillborn infant. Each time I returned to this subject, Stefa offered the same response with the resolution of one who has determined to take a secret along to the grave. I wasn't all that concerned. The child, if it existed at all, was Mark's, not mine. One of the womanizers at the Writers' Club had once given me a list of symptoms by which to determine if a woman had ever given birth. Later, a gynecologist I had met on vacation told me that all these alleged signs were pure nonsense.

I was ashamed of my curiosity and tried somehow to justify it, but Stefa gave me no opportunity to do so. She seized my wrist, cast a solemn look at me, and said, "I have a daughter!"

I had the feeling that the words had been torn from her mouth.

"Where is she?"

"In Gdansk."

Stefa didn't let go of my hand but squeezed it forcefully, as if waiting for me to ask more.

"Leon knows?"

"Yes, he knows. He pays for her. He even wanted to bring her to Warsaw, but I didn't want our families to have something to gossip about forever. My father is alive and I don't want to cause him grief. He will never know that he has a grandchild. Mark's mother died without this satisfaction. Nor does Mark know that he's a father. I've wanted to speak to you about this on many occasions, but somehow I always postponed it. The Nazis are on the verge of seizing Gdansk and the whole Corridor. I don't want my child to fall into the hands of those murderers."

"If they seize Gdansk, they can seize Warsaw too," I said, not sure whether I should say this and for what purpose.

"Yes, true, but Leon is an optimist—so deeply involved in his business that he is blind to all other matters. He keeps predicting that it will never come to war. In his own fashion, Leon is a good person. If only I could love him—but something about him repels me. The worst of it is that I absolutely cannot understand him. His whole way of thinking and all his emotions are those of someone who has come down from another planet. His whole being is focused on money, yet he gets little pleasure from all his earnings. He loves me, but in a way as if I were a bargain he had caught at some bazaar."

"If he loves you, convince him to get your daughter and take you both to America."

"That he wouldn't do. He's even afraid to go to the country for the summer. When he took that trip around the world with me, he claimed to have lost half of his fortune because of it. He remains in the city during the worst heat waves. It's gotten so I myself don't want to go anywhere anymore. Not with him. When he's away from Warsaw and his business, he becomes completely mad."

"Why don't you have a child together?"

"Oh, I don't want his child. I don't want any more children. What for? I shouldn't say this, but the older Franka gets—I named my daughter after my dead aunt —the more she resembles Mark. The German woman who is bringing her up keeps sending photographs, and her resemblance to him is uncanny. If I were raising her myself perhaps I might not notice this so clearly, but when I receive the photos I see things a mother shouldn't see. I still hope to God that she won't have his character. Oh, you shouldn't have asked me about it, then I wouldn't have had to say these bitter words. My love for Mark has changed into revulsion. Once I found a photograph of him among my papers and when I looked at it I literally threw up."

"Where is he?"

"I don't know and I don't want to know. You are, in a sense, the witness to my fiasco—to all my fiascoes. Because he was so passionately assimilated, I grew closer to Jewishness, but I can't stand the Jews either. The whole species of man is revolting to me. I ask no favor of God, but I would like my father to die in his sleep. That's an easy death. Then I would put an end to the whole rottenness."

CHAPTER THREE

I

I had packed my clothes and my manuscripts into the two valises that I took with me to America. I said goodbye to Aaron Zeitlin, to J. J. Trunk, and to a few others. The Jewish section of the PEN Club was issuing my first book in Yiddish, *Satan in Goray,* but copies weren't yet ready for me to take along.

Stefa, Leon Treitler, and my cousin Esther came to see me off at the railroad station. They had wanted to make a farewell party for me at the Writers' Club, but I demurred. I had observed many such parties. The writers ate, drank tea, and made long and often inane speeches about the guest of honor. The wags made quiet fun of the speakers and of their silly praises. I had occasionally been one of those wags and more than once I had heard some hack being praised in superlatives. The speakers often justified this by claiming that they had done it out of compassion for a neglected writer, a foreign visitor, or whoever he might have been. I wasn't anxious to be a part of this sort of literary philanthropy. I was already close to thirty and all I had accomplished in Yiddish literature was one novella and several short stories that I had published in magazines and anthologies no one read. I had seen writers, actors, and other creative people literally arrange banquets and jubilees in their own behalf. Long before they reached the age of fifty, they began mentioning the date of their birth, or the date of their first publication, or appearing on the stage, hinting and grumbling about the lack of public appreciation. Invariably, a group of friends evolved who did recognize and did remember. Sometimes a "surprise" banquet was then arranged for the forgotten hero, who wrote the invitations himself. I recall one time when they tried to enlist J. J. Trunk in such a masquerade, but he had enough sense to decline. "It's not that I dislike honor," he told me, "but I refuse shame."

In a way, the last few weeks prior to my departure were to me like a long holiday. People were friendlier to me than ever, often sentimental, as if sensing that we would never see each other again. Women with whom I had conducted semi-, quarter-, or might-have-been affairs suddenly determined that this was the time for us to go further or all the way.

In those days, a trip to America was still considered an adventure. True, Lindbergh had already flown the Atlantic, but passenger service to America was still by sea. My biggest concern was that as a single passenger I would have to share a cabin with another man. My need for privacy was so strong that I was ready to spend my last groschen for a private cabin. The fact is that even my last groschen wouldn't have helped. I confided my predicament to my travel agent and he was astounded that I should be perturbed about such a trifle.

At that time the famed French ship the *Normandie* was scheduled to make her maiden voyage to New York. All the snobs of Europe strove to be aboard. My agent himself was booked to make this voyage. He had become so friendly with me that he suggested that I wait two weeks and share his cabin on the *Normandie*. But I declined the privilege. First of all, I feared an imminent Hitler invasion; but mainly I still hoped to get a private cabin aboard some other vessel. After a lengthy search, the agent located what I had been seeking—a cabin for one, without portholes and also without air, on a French ship.

Everything was over—the frantic words, the kisses, the embraces, the fervent promises to bring over almost everyone I knew to America even though all I held was a six-month tourist visa. It was the month of April, 1935. The following day was the birthday of one of the most cruel murderers in world history, Hitler. I had to travel by train through Nazi Germany because it would have been too expensive to take a different route. I had heard that Jewish passengers were forced to get off the train and they were searched and subjected to other indignities. I would be proceeding directly into the hands of the evildoers. They could easily take away my passport and visa and send me to a concentration camp. I fully grasped the danger, but somehow fear within me had gone into a kind of hibernation, to be replaced by a sense of fatalism.

I stood by the window of the coach looking out at the

lights of Warsaw, and what I saw appeared as strange to me as if I were seeing it for the first time. Soon the lights of the city faded and in the semidarkness emerged factories, and structures that were hard to identify. Only the glowing sky gave evidence that we weren't far from a large city.

This international train had sleeping cars and a diner. I traveled tourist-class, which was better lit than the usual third-class car and had more comfortable seats. Three Chinese men sat facing me and conversed in their language. Or maybe they were Koreans? This was the first time I had been that close to people of another race. I had seen several Orientals in Warsaw, and once, a black man, but always from afar, perhaps through a streetcar window.

Although we were still close to Warsaw and the train ran past little depots of familiar towns, I felt as if I were already abroad. I knew that I would never come this way again and that Warsaw, Poland, the Writers' Club, my mother, my brother Moishe, and the women who were near to me had all passed over into the sphere of memory. The fact is that they had been ghosts even while I was still with them. Long before I ever heard of Berkeley and Kant, I felt that what we call reality had no substance other than that formed in our minds. I was, one might say, a solipsist long before I ever heard of the word; actually, from the day I commenced pondering the so-called eternal questions.

There had been moments when I had assumed that once I got the visa to America I would be happy. But I felt no happiness now, not even a trace. I was glad somehow that the passengers on the other bench didn't know my language so that I wouldn't have to converse with them.

I sat by the window looking out at the dense darkness, and from time to time, glanced up at the stars. I wasn't leaving *them*. The universe rode along with me. I recognized the shapes of the constellations. Perhaps the universe accompanied us on our journey into eternity when we concluded the little incident we call life?

I stretched out on the seat and from time to time I fingered the passport inside my breast pocket. "Up there, there are no borders, no passports," the babbler within me babbled. "There are no Nazis. Could a star be a Nazi? Up there, there is no lack of living space. Up there—let us hope—you don't have to fight for your existence if you exist."

I toyed with my thoughts like a child playing with knucklebones. By dawn, we had reached the border. There was a change of conductors. I saw a man wearing a swastika. He took my passport and turned its pages. He asked how much money I was carrying and I told him and showed him the bank notes. He said, "Not necessary," and returned the passport. Another individual wearing a swastika came in and the two exchanged a salutation: "Heil Hitler!" Then they left.

I saw through a window Jews being herded inside a building to be searched. I later heard that some had been stripped naked. We had entered the land of the Inquisition.

As in all other inquisitions, the sun remained neutral. It rose and its light illuminated balconies decorated with Nazi banners. It was the Führer's forty-seventh birthday. I forgot to mention that all this occurred during the intermediary days of Passover. Leon Treitler had invited me to the seder. Stefa had prepared matzohs, the bitter herbs, as well as fish, meat, and matzohballs. Leon Treitler had donned a white robe and recited the Haggada. I had asked the Four Questions. None of us took the ceremony too seriously. None of us believed the miracle of the Exodus from Egypt and the parting of the Red Sea. Stefa's father had declined to attend the seder at his daughter's home. He didn't trust her *kashruth*. He probably didn't want to see me either.

I don't recall if we rode the same train the whole way or if we changed trains at the border. In Berlin a young man came into the car and called my name. I became frightened. Had they come to arrest me? It turned out that the young man worked for (or was associated with) my travel agent and he brought me some matzohs and a Passover delicacy. At that time the persecutions of the Jews in Germany had just commenced. The other passengers looked on in amazement as I sat chewing the matzoh. The day was sunny and balmy, and outside of the flags with the swastikas, one couldn't tell that the country was in the hands of a savage dictator. German families sat out on balconies eating lunch. Their faces appeared genial. The streets in the cities and towns that we rode through were clean and almost empty. Someone had left a German newspaper on the seat and I read an enthusiastic article about Hitler; about what he had already accomplished and what he would do for Germany in the future.

Late at night the train stopped at the Belgian border and I had to show my passport again. This was my second sleepless night and I no longer had any curiosity about the country through which we were passing. I lay on the hard bench and stopped trying to straighten my limbs. My half-muffled ears heard conversations in French and Flemish.

I had resolved not to become too excited over Paris, like all the others. Someone at the Writers' Club had given me the address of a cheap hotel in a section called Belleville. I was scheduled to spend two or three days in Paris, then take the train to Cherbourg, where my ship was docked. In the thirty-six hours I had been traveling, I had accustomed myself to the enforced sleeplessness, to eating meals from a paper bag, to not exchanging a word with anyone, and not changing my clothes. I didn't even glance at the stamps that the border officials affixed to my passport. I made no effort to study those who got on and off in the various countries. I had grown indifferent to the notion of traveling abroad, which had once been my dream.

Day started breaking and rain was falling. We were already in France and the train was approaching Paris. I thought about the travelers of earlier days who had to endure long journeys in stagecoaches, carriages, even on horseback. Where did they gather the strength and the patience for so many hardships? Why hadn't they sooner chosen to stay home?

I had dozed and yawned. The conductor prodded my shoulder. We had arrived in Paris. I felt my breast pocket, where I kept my passport and the ship's ticket, and the trouser back pocket, where I kept my money, some fifty dollars in American and French bank notes. Then I seized the two valises, which seemed to have grown heavier. The taxi driver didn't understand me and I handed him the slip of paper with the address written on it. He glanced at it and shook his head. Although I had told him that I understood no French, he began speaking the unfamiliar language, perhaps to himself. It seemed to me that he was saying, "Of all the respectable passengers, I had to catch such a piker as you."

He whistled and began driving the car recklessly fast. It was still raining and the people out in the streets were of the type that cruise cities at dawn simply to prove that they can overcome all hardships. They crossed the streets oblivious to all signs and warnings. They seemed to say mutely, "If you want to run me over, go to it." The taxi driver blared his horn and abused them with what sounded like foul language in French. From time to time he turned to look back at me as if to make sure that I hadn't jumped out during the ride.

Despite all this, I was overcome with a strong affection for this city. It exuded a serenity I had never experienced before. I felt the mute presence of generations of inhabitants who were both dead and alive, remote and near, unearthly sad and also gay, full of ghostly wisdom and divine resignation. I sensed the very danger I had resolved to avoid—falling in love with Paris at first sight, as so many enthusiasts had done before me. Every street, every house had its individual allure—not one artificial or planned, but that originality that evolves by itself out of genuine talent, a harmony that no one can imitate. Every roof, chimney, balcony, window, shutter, door, and lamppost suited the complete image. Even the shabby pedestrians seemed oddly appropriate to the scene. The deceased who had left this rich inheritance were watching.

We drove into a street and the taxi stopped. I took out the French bank notes and the driver peeled off the amount coming to him, or perhaps more. At the same time he mumbled to himself and winked, mocking my helplessness.

A female concierge led me up five flights of stairs to a garret room with a wide brass bed and a sink. The rain had stopped and the sun had come out. Across the narrow street a girl stood and beat a worn rug with a stick. On the pavement nearby a pigeon hopped on its red feet, pecking at what looked to me like a pebble. The fact that the creature didn't flee from someone waving a stick and making noise struck me as strange. Windows were thrown open by half-naked women and radios chattered, droned, whistled, played music, sang. I had never heard such sweet tones, such lighthearted melodies. Two prostitutes conversed from window to window and called down to men in the streets. I fell back onto the brass bed and sank into a deep sleep.

Unbelievably, someone knew of my arrival in Paris and came to take me to breakfast and show me the city. Paris had its own Yiddish Writers' Club. Someone at the Warsaw Writers' Club had apparently alerted the local club members to my arrival. I couldn't believe my sleepy eyes. No one had ever granted me such an honor. The small, dark youth addressed me in a tone one would employ toward an older writer. He had read my stories in *The Literary Weekly* and in *Globus,* he said. He knew that the PEN Club was issuing my book. He was five years younger than I, and he had already published several poems in the Yiddish newspapers in Paris. For a moment I thought he was confusing me with my brother, but it turned out he knew about both my brother and about myself. He proposed an interview with me for a Paris Yiddish newspaper.

The weather had turned warm and my guide told me

that I wouldn't be needing my overcoat. We walked down the five flights of stairs and went outside. The street was crowded with people and they all spoke Yiddish. Many carried the local Communist Yiddish newspaper, others the paper of the Labor Zionist Party. I recognized several of the Communists who used to visit the Writers' Club in Warsaw. The Yiddishist world was a small town. They came up to me and greeted me coldly. They asked, "What's the fascist Pilsudski up to? Is he still alive?" They gathered in little cliques here just as they had in the Writers' Club in Warsaw. Their eyes flowed with sly triumph. Mussolini had just attacked or seized Ethiopia. The worse conditions became, the better grew the chances for the world revolution. Each one of them was grooming himself to be not less than a commissar. I asked my guide how these Warsaw Communists survived in France, and he told me that there were wealthy Jews in Paris who supported them. They reckoned that this would save them when the day of avenge came.

He took me to a restaurant and it smelled just the same as the Jewish restaurants in Warsaw, Cracow, Vilna, and Gdansk. Patrons ate chicken soup with noodles and conversed across the tables. A small man with a huge head scribbled figures on a tablecloth. A man in black-rimmed glasses went from table to table issuing cards attesting to the fact that he became crippled in a Polish prison and was in need of financial aid. After a while he came back to collect the cards and any coins the guest might have donated. At almost every table they discussed the peace conference that the Communists were planning to convene, as well as the merits of a united front. A Yiddish writer from America, Zachariah Kammermacher, came up to me and asked, "What are *you* doing here?"

I recognized him from the photograph that the editor of *The Literary Weekly* had published. He had been both for the Communists and against them. He agreed with them on certain points and disagreed on others. As he spoke to me he gestured with his thumb. One eye looked up, the other down. He had written a poem in which he compared Rosa Luxemburg to Mother Rachel. He considered himself a Zionist, but he was also against Zionism and sought a territory in Australia or South America where the Jews could settle. Essentially, he had confided to me, he was a religious anarchist. He had come to Paris now to arrange the peace conference and, at the same time, to organize a commission to study the Jewish question the world over. He was awaiting a meeting with Leon Blum. Some words he enunciated clearly, others he snorted through his nose. My guide remarked to me later, "One thing you can be sure—he didn't come here at his own expense."

"Who pays for him then?"

"Someone pays. He is so immersed in politics that he's

no longer a writer. I tried to read him once and I couldn't make head or tail of a single sentence."

2

I settled back in the train taking me from Paris to Cherbourg. The day was a sunny one, but my spirit was blighted by my own broodings and by everything I had seen and heard around me. My pious forebears called this world the world of lies, and the graveyard they called the world of truth. I was preparing to be a writer in that world of lies, eager to add my own portion of falsehood. But the trees bloomed, the birds sang, each with its own tune. Cool breezes wafted in from somewhere, carrying scents that intoxicated me. I had an urge (actually, a fantasy) to spring down from the train and lose myself in the green vegetation where every leaf, every blade of grass and fly and worm was a divine masterpiece. Even the peasant huts nearby appeared to be the product of some unique artistic instinct. I slept over in Cherbourg in a hotel arranged for me by the shipping line. That night is totally erased from my memory. All I can remember of this hotel is that it contained a sink with hot and cold running water; I had never before seen anything like this in Poland except in a public bath.

The next day, I boarded the ship, they took my ticket, and my pockets felt empty. All I had there now was my passport. I had been left practically penniless. Thank

God, I didn't have to share my cabin with anyone. My two valises stood in the dark cabin, silent witnesses that I had lived nearly thirty years in Poland, which that day seemed to me more remote than it does now, forty years later. I was what the cabala calls a naked soul—a soul which has departed one body and awaits another. This trip made me forget so many facts and faces that I began to suspect that I was becoming senile. Or was it a temporary attack of amnesia? Was this what happened to the soul directly following death? Was Purah, the Angel of Forgetfulness, also the Angel of Death? I wanted to make a notation of this thought in my notebook but I had forgotten to take it along.

The ship remained in the harbor for many hours, but I stayed in my windowless cabin, which was illuminated by a small electric lamp. I heard running in the passageway, talk. The other passengers had friends seeing them off. They drank, snapped pictures. People quickly struck up friendships. I heard foreign languages. I had dozed off, and when I opened my eyes, I sensed a vibration under the mattress upon which I was lying. I went out on the deck. Evening had fallen and the sun had gone down. Cherbourg faded in the distance. Those on deck gazed at me with a kind of surprise, as if asking themselves, "What's *he* doing here?" A tall individual in a checkered suit, knickers, and a white cyclist's cap, and with a camera hanging from his shoulder, paced to and fro, taking long strides. He greeted the ladies, addressing them in English and French. Men of such height were rarely seen in Poland, and certainly not among the Jews. His square-jawed face seemed to say, This is my world, my ship, my women. Suddenly it occurred to me that I had forgotten the number of my cabin. I was supposed to have taken the key to my cabin with me but I had apparently left it inside. I had lost the stub of my ticket, too. I tried to locate my cabin without the help of others (who could have helped me?) but I only strayed through the passageways and climbed up and down countless stairs. I tried to seek someone's assistance and I stopped a member of the crew, but he knew only French. I traveled in circles, like a jackass around a millstone. Every few minutes I saw the same faces. The passengers apparently divined my confusion, since they smiled and winked at each other. My demons had not abandoned me. They were accompanying me to America.

I climbed a staircase to where a long line of passengers stood before a window where an official marked something down on cards for them. I heard a woman in the line speaking German and after some hesitation I asked her what the people were waiting for. She explained to me that this concerned seating arrangements. I told the woman that I had forgotten my cabin number and she said, "It's easy enough to find out. Ask the purser." I wanted to ask her where the "purser" could be located but at that moment a man came up and began talking to her. Was it possible that I would spend the entire eight days of the journey searching for my cabin? It's but a single step from neurosis to insanity, I admonished myself. The woman had mentioned something about a first or second sitting but I didn't understand what this meant. Still, I took a place in the line. If you won't have a place to sleep, I said to myself, at least assure yourself of food. One could spend the night on the stairs. I knew full well that my nerves required suspense and I had to create it. Whenever I became overly excited, irritated, lonesome, the anxieties of my childhood returned to me with all their daydreams, false assumptions, ridiculous suspicions, superstitions. I lost my sense of direction completely. I stopped recognizing people, I made flagrant mistakes in speaking. Some mocking demon began to play games with me and even though I realized it was all sham and nonsense I had to cooperate.

I had reached the official issuing the cards and informed him that I understood only German. He began speaking German to me, but in such an accent that I couldn't figure out what he was saying. How is this possible? I had translated a half-dozen books from German. Was he speaking in slang? Or had I lost my mind? He considered a moment, then handed me a card: "second sitting." He might have been a Nazi who had signed on this ship to spy on the passengers and, possibly, to torment Jews. This card might be a signal to the waiter to poison my food. Suddenly, I recalled the number of my cabin. I went to look for it and located it immediately. The door was not locked. I had left the key on the table. My two valises stood where I had left them. I grasped what was meant by the term "sittings"—the time at which breakfast, lunch, and dinner were served. It was good that he gave me the second sitting. Otherwise, I would have been forced to get up at 7 A.M.

I changed my clothes—I had only one other suit— then went out on deck. Cherbourg had vanished from sight. To the best of my recollection, the moon wasn't out that evening, but the sky was thickly sprinkled with stars. They appeared to me lower than on land and somehow bigger. They didn't remain fixed, but bobbed and swayed with the ship. Somewhere a lighthouse cast beams of light.

Here, heaven and earth weren't separate and distant from each other but merged into a single cosmic entity, endowed with an otherworldly light. I stood in the center of the universe, the ferment that hadn't abated since Genesis and perhaps even long before that, because according to the Bible the abyss and the divine breath had preceded Creation. A solemnity hovered over it all, blue, prediurnal. The sound of the waves fused into a monotonous roar, a seething, a foaming, a splashing that didn't weary the ear or the brain. God spoke a single word, awesome and eternal.

The waves assaulted the ship in an arc, locked it in a watery dance, ready to suck it in within their vortex, but at the last moment they retreated like maneuvering armies, prepared to commence their war games again. Creation played with the sea, the stars, the ship, with the little human beings bustling about within its innards. My despair had begun to fade gradually. There was no room for suffering in the midst of this celestial frolic. All my worries were insignificant and groundless to begin with. Who did it concern whether I managed to accomplish anything or nothing? Nothing itself became an essence. I stood there until my watch showed that it was time for the second sitting.

I went down to my cabin and headed for the dining hall. The people in the first sitting hadn't yet finished eating, but a crowd already stood by the door, ready to rush inside and grab their places the moment the first sitting was concluded. Were all these people really so hungry? And which of them would turn out to be my dinner partners? How would I communicate with them? I was the last to enter. The headwaiter, or whatever his title may have been, glanced at my card and his face expressed something akin to astonishment. He flipped the card over and looked at its other side as if expecting to find there the solution to the puzzle. He arched his brows and shrugged. Then everything appeared to have become clear to him and he said in a clear German, "There is only one single table in the whole dining room and it's been assigned to you. If you're reluctant to sit alone, we can ignore the card and seat you with those close to you. Maybe you'd prefer the kosher table? You'd surely find agreeable companions there."

"I thank you very much," I replied, "but a table for one is actually what I'd like."

"You prefer isolation, eh? Your table is in a corner. We occasionally have passengers who choose to eat alone. On the last trip, there was a priest, a missionary, or God knows what he was. He demanded his own table and we accommodated him. Come."

He led the way through the crowded hall and I noticed that hardly anyone here was alone. English was spoken, French, Italian, German. How long ago was it that they had waged war? How long ago did they drop bombs on each other? But all that was forgotten. Some passengers were already seated, with that air of assurance of those who always belong where they are. I didn't see one shy face. Women laughed that world-affirming laughter that has no connection with humor but rather with something bosomy, fleshy, abdominal. The men seemed as earthy and as anxious to strike up friendships as the women. Finally, we reached my table. It stood in a corner and somehow off balance, crooked, between two walls and two tables, the diners of which stared at me in a kind of amazement that seemed to ask, "Why was *he* picked as the victim?" My chair was a narrow one and I barely managed to squeeze myself into it. From where I sat I could see practically the entire hall, but my eyes had grown so bedazzled that I saw everything as if through a dense mist. After a long while a waiter came over and said, "Your order, please?"

Oddly, I had for years contemplated becoming a vegetarian. I had actually gone through periods during which I had eaten no animal flesh. But I often had to eat on credit at the Writers' Club, and I lacked the courage to demand special dishes. I had put it all aside for the time when I could act according to my convictions. Abruptly now, I blurted, "I am very sorry, but I'm a vegetarian."

The waiter shook his head. "We don't have a special vegetarian kitchen. You were told that you could eat at the kosher table, but you refused."

"Those who are kosher aren't vegetarians," I told him. My voice had grown so weak that he had to bring his ear close to my lips to hear me.

"Eh? But there is some kind of connection there." His tone grew more genial. "I understand all your motives, but our kitchen simply isn't geared for such exceptions."

"You needn't make any exceptions. Be so good as to bring me whatever you want and I'll eat only those things I'm allowed."

"Do you eat eggs? Milk?"

"Yes."

"Well, in the eight days you're aboard the ship, you

won't starve. We have bread, butter, many good cheeses and egg dishes."

"I'll be satisfied with whatever you bring me."

Immediately, questions came at me from the tables among which I was squeezed. Some people addressed me in French, some in English, some in German. What was the reason for my vegetarianism? Was it on account of my health? On doctors' orders? Did it have to do with my religion? The men appeared insulted that I had introduced a sort of controversy into their presence. They had come here to enjoy themselves, not to philosophize about the anguish of animals and fish. I tried in my mangled German to explain to them that my vegetarianism was based on no religion but simply on the feeling that one creature lacked the right to rob another creature of its life and devour it. I turned momentarily and against my will, propagandist.

"What right have we to curtail a life that God has granted? The animal in the forest and the fish in the water have done us no harm."

A man with a stern face said to me, "If you allowed the animals and birds to multiply, they'd eat up all the grain in our fields. I myself live in a region where deer roam. It's forbidden to hunt them out of season and it's happened not once but ten times that they ate all the plants in my garden. You're allowed to hunt them a few months in the year only, but no matter how many are shot, it isn't enough. Well, and what would you do about the hares and rabbits and birds? The Department of Agriculture has just now advised that the hunters should shoot at least thirty crows a day. Otherwise, America would become a land not of plenty but of famine. Do you know all this? Did you ever read a book about such matters?"

"No, I don't know. But at least we should leave the fish alone. They stay in the water in their own element. They don't come out on land to devour our crops."

"They don't, eh? In certain lakes in America, the fish have multiplied to such a degree that they allow themselves to be caught with bare hands. Creatures have instinct and they know that when they overmultiply they must perish. . . . Here is our waiter."

One waiter brought a magnum of champagne and another a tray that he balanced overhead. They seemed as excited as the people they served. One opened the champagne with a pop, let a man taste it before pouring for the ladies. The other served the plates of appetizers. For a while it appeared that the waiter would ignore me completely. He didn't even glance into the corner where I sat. But soon he seemed to have reminded himself and he remarked, "There will be something for you too."

And he ran off with his tray.

CHAPTER FOUR

I

In past years I had grown accustomed to meeting strangers. Once in a while readers approached to pay me compliments for an article or a story. I had girl friends and a few other friends among the writers. I had established the minimum contact necessary for existence. But aboard this ship my sense of solitude came flooding back in all its magnitude. My neighbors in the dining hall had apparently resolved to leave me to myself. I greeted them but they didn't respond. I don't know to this day if it was my vegetarianism that put them into a hostile mood or the fact that I chose to sit alone. The waiter did bring me food but it seemed to be made up of leftovers he had collected: mostly stale bread, an occasional chunk of cheese, an onion, a carrot. I had committed the sin of isolating myself from others, and I had been excommunicated. Each diner was served a carafe of wine daily, but I got no wine. Much as I brooded about this treatment, I could never come to accept it. One thing I knew for certain, I was at fault, not they. Eating in the dining hall became so annoying to me that I proposed to the waiter that he serve me in my cabin. He grew angry, glared, then told me to go to a certain office with a name I

couldn't pronounce. This must have been on the third day of my trip, but I felt as if I had been already swaying on this ship for weeks.

After lengthy questioning and straying, I made my way to the office where a small man sat scratching away at a sheet of paper with a pen that reminded me of my days in cheder. It consisted of a wooden holder, a ferrule, and the steel pen itself. The point looked old, rusty, broken. Every few seconds the writer dipped the pen in an inkwell that seemed nearly empty. The ink appeared dense and it kept spotting. Even in Warsaw such a pen would have been an anachronism. The sheet of paper was unlined and the writing emerged so crooked that each line rode piggyback upon the next. I cleared my throat and spoke some of the French words I knew— *"Monsieur, s'il vous plaît"*—but the other didn't react at all. Had my voice grown so quiet or was he deaf? This, I told myself, was a French Akaki Akakevich, a throwback to Gogol's times. I forced myself to wait patiently, but a good half hour went by and he still didn't give the slightest indication that someone was waiting for him. I noticed that he was coming close to the bottom of the long sheet and this gave some hope. And that's how it was. The moment he had written the last crooked line and blotted it with an ancient blotter, he raised his head and looked at me with eyes that could have belonged to a fish, totally devoid of expression. They were spaced far apart. He had a short, broad nose and a wide mouth. He appeared to have just wakened from a deep sleep or a trance. I started explaining to him in German, in Yiddish, and with my few words of French, the nature of my request, but his pale eyes gazed at me without any comprehension.

I said several times, "*Je manger en kabine,* no restaurant."

He gathered my meaning finally, for after protracted searching he handed me a card and asked me to sign it. Then he gave me another card. The ship had agreed to provide me board in my own cabin. I asked him in sign language what to do with this card and as far as I could determine the answer was, "Hold on to it."

From that day on I was going to America as if on a prison ship—a windowless cabin with little air—and with food brought by a man who could be a prison guard. He never knocked but barged right in, kicking the door open with his foot. He slammed down the tray without a word. If a book or a manuscript was lying on the little table, he inevitably drenched it. I tried several times to speak to him, at least to learn his name, but he never responded. He looked to me to be a native of the French colonies.

The food he brought me was always the same. In the morning—bread with black coffee. For lunch—some groats with no wine or dessert. For dinner—he threw me a piece of stale bread, some cheese, and a kind of white

sausage I had never before seen in Poland. My order for vegetarian food was ignored. He never even glanced at me. I tried to give him a tip but he wouldn't touch the bank note.

I knew already how impossible it was to explain the human character and its whims. Still, as I lay nights on the hard mattress, which was apparently located directly over the ship's engine, I tried to deduce the reason for his surly behavior. Did he despise the white man and his civilization? Was the act of bringing me food three times a day too strenuous for him? Did he resent those who demanded special privileges? Because I threw away the meat he brought me, I actually subsisted on stale bread and cheese. The black coffee was never more than a half cup, cold and bitter. I knew that I would arrive in America (assuming they let me in, considering my appearance) looking wasted.

I had a number of choices of how to improve my lot. First, I didn't have to spend all my time inside my dark cell. The steward on deck rented folding chairs and I could sit all day sunning myself in the fresh air. Second, the ship had a library. True, most of the books were in French, but there were several in German. But some force kept me from doing what was best for me. Somehow, I had acquired a fear of the sun and its light. The deck was too crowded with people. There was a place to play badminton, and young men ran, shouted, often put their arms around the women. I had taken from the ship's library a German translation of Ilya Ehrenburg, but somehow I couldn't take the impudent style of one who assumed that only he was clever while the rest of the world was made up of idiots.

It was the fifth day of the journey. In three days I would be landing in New York. I had finally dared to rent a chair on the deck and I had another book from the ship's library that I was anxious to read. It was a German translation of Bergson's *Creative Evolution*. I also carried with me a Yiddish magazine in which I had published my latest story before I left Poland. I was so engrossed in Bergson's work that for a while I forgot about my spiritual crisis. One didn't have to be a professional philosopher to realize that Bergson was a talented writer, a *Schöngeist*, not a philosopher. This was an elegant book, interestingly written, but lacking any new concepts. *"Élan vital"* is a pretty phrase, but Bergson didn't even try to explain how it came to be a creative power. I had already grown accustomed to works that evoke a sensation of originality at the beginning only to find that when the reader reaches the last page he is just as wise as he had been at the first. There had been many vitalists among biologists prior to Bergson, even prior to Lamarck.

As I sat there reading, a steward came up escorting a young woman. There was an empty chair next to mine and he seated her in it. He carefully covered her legs with a blanket, then brought her a cup of bouillon. He offered me the same but I declined. It was hard to determine my neighbor's age. She might have been in her late twenties or early thirties. She also held a book—Baudelaire's *Fleurs du Mal* bound in velvet. She wore a white blouse and a gray skirt. Her dark complexion was pitted from acne. I read on for a long time. I didn't have the slightest urge to talk to her. She probably spoke only French. I still tried to grasp how the *élan vital* could have created or formed the sky, the stars, the sea, and Bergson himself and his beautiful phrases and illusions. For a long time we each read our books. Then she turned toward me and said in a halting Warsaw Yiddish, "You're reading a book I always wanted to read but somehow I never did. Is it really as interesting as it seems?"

I was so surprised that I forgot to be embarrassed. "You speak Yiddish!"

"I see that you read Yiddish." And she pointed at my magazine.

"Yiddish is my mother language."

"Mine, too," she said in Polish. "Until I was seven I knew no other language but Yiddish."

"You undoubtedly come from an Orthodox home."

"Yes, but . . ."

I sat quietly and waited for her to go on. For the first time in five days, someone was speaking to me. I said, "You speak Polish without a trace of a Jewish accent."

"Do you really think so? My feeling is that my Polish sounds foreign."

"At least your parents had the wisdom to send you to a secular school," I said. "My father sent me to cheder and that was the only source of my education."

"What was he—a Chasid?"

"A rabbi, a *moreh horoah,* if you know what that means."

"I know. I was brought up in the same kind of household as you, but something happened that turned everything upside down for us."

"May I ask what happened?"

She didn't answer immediately and seemed to hesitate. I was about to tell her that she need not reply when she said, "My father was a pious Jew. He wore a beard, earlocks, and a long gabardine like all the others. He was a Talmud teacher. My mother wore a wig. I often demanded of my father that he send me to a Polish school, but he always postponed this with all sorts of pretexts. But something was going on in our house. I was an only child. My two brothers and one sister died before I was born. At night I often heard my father screaming and my mother crying. I began to suspect that my parents wanted to divorce. One evening when I came home and asked Mother where Father was, she told me that he had left for England. I had often heard that men on our street—we lived in the very midst of poverty, on Smocza Street—went off to America. But England seemed to me even farther away than America. On Smocza Street if you wanted to say that someone was acting strange, you said he was acting 'English.' I'll make it short—my father converted, became a member of the Church of England and a missionary. Strange, isn't it?"

"Yes, strange. What was his name?"

"Nathan Fishelzohn. He didn't change his name."

"I knew Nathan Fishelzohn," I said.

"You knew him?"

"I visited him once in his chapel on Krolewska Street."

"Oh, my God. When I saw you with that Yiddish magazine, I thought that—many young men used to visit him. Did you even intend to . . . ?"

"No. I went to see him just out of curiosity, not alone but with a friend of his who is also my friend, a Yiddish writer, Dr. Gliksman."

"I know Dr. Gliksman. What a small world! Are you a Yiddish writer?"

"I try to be."

"May I ask your name?"

I told her my name.

"My name is Zofia now, or Zosia. It used to be Reitze Gitl. Did you write *Yoshe Kalb?*"

"No, my older brother did."

"This book just came out in Polish translation. I read it. So did my father. Really, the big world is a small village!"

And for a long while we both looked at one another in silence. Then she continued, "Smocza Street, as you know, is full of Jews. The only gentiles around were the janitors in every courtyard. Ours would come around every Friday for his ten groschen. To hear that my father had become a *goy* was such a shock that I really have no words for it. When they learned on Smocza Street that our family had converted, the boys threw stones at me. Girls spat at me. They smashed our windows. Then the mission bought a house on Krolewska Street and we all moved in there. Some rich lady in England had left a fortune to have Jesus brought to the Polish Jews. There I started attending a school where all lessons were taught in English except for the Polish language and Polish history. But my parents continued to converse in Yiddish. . . . Why am I telling you all this? I noticed you from the very first day you boarded the ship. You seemed strangely lost. Each time I saw you, you weren't walking but running, as if you were being chased."

"May I ask what you intend to do in America?"

"A good question. I don't know. I don't know myself. Ever since the rise of Hitlerism, our school in Warsaw began to become strongly anti-Semitic. Later I was attending the Warsaw university, but somehow I lost interest. You mustn't laugh at what I'm about to tell you, but I write too. I have a letter of recommendation to a lady professor at Radcliffe, however, I'm not sure I want to continue my studies in general. I made two visits to England. I hoped to study there, even settle there, but I soon realized that to them I would always be a Jewess from Poland. There if you don't speak with an Oxford accent and you don't have an earl for a grandfather, you don't belong. I guess you aren't a religious Jew in the accepted sense of the word either."

"Far from it."

"They assigned me a cabin with two Englishwomen and they're making me crazy with their silly talk. For whom do you write? For Jews who read Yiddish?"

"Yes, those are my readers."

"I tried reading a translation from Peretz, but it didn't capture my interest. I liked Bialik better, but he is kind of primitive too. My father reads all the Yiddish books. As soon as a Yiddish book comes out, he reads it. I'm certain that he has read you. Where does your brother live? In Warsaw?"

"He is now in America. It's to him that I'm going."

"Does he have a family?"

"Yes, a wife and child."

"Well, it's a small world, and particularly so, the Jewish world. One time in my life I had one ambition—to tear myself away from this world as firmly as possible. I dreamed of discovering a planet where the word 'Jew' had never been heard. What evil did the Jews commit that one must be so ashamed of them? It was they who were burned by the Inquisition—they didn't burn others. Now that Naziism has evolved, Christians of Jewish descent face the same danger as do the Jews on Smocza Street. Really, at times it seems to me that I'm living in one great insane asylum."

"That's what it is."

"What do you write about? Where do you eat? I seldom see you in the dining room."

I had to tell Zosia about my dark cabin and the man who threw me my bread and cheese with such resentment thrice daily, and she said:

"Come eat with me. My table is half empty. There is only one elderly couple there. He is a retired captain of a freighter owned by a fruit company. He and his wife are both quiet people but they are alcoholics. When they come down for breakfast mornings, they are both already drunk. They're so drunk that they can't speak properly. They stutter and mumble. They hardly eat a thing. The waiter would be pleased to have you at his table."

"I don't have a number for this table."

"No one asks for any numbers. Many of the passengers are seasick and they don't show up at the dining room."

"I'm a vegetarian."

"What? You'll get whatever you ask for. There's no reason for you to lock yourself up in a self-imposed prison."

That evening I joined Zosia at her table. I got a rich vegetarian meal. I even drank two glasses of wine. The elderly couple gave me a friendly reception. The husband, the ex-captain, muttered something inarticulately to me. I told him that I didn't know English but this didn't stop him from rambling on.

I asked Zosia what he was saying and she replied in Polish, "I don't understand him myself."

His wife seemed somewhat less drunk. After a while, the couple left the table. The old woman was suffering from seasickness. She suddenly grew nauseous. The husband tried to keep her from falling but his own legs were wobbly.

Zosia observed to me in Yiddish, "Now you can speak to me in the mother tongue."

"I don't believe in miracles," I said, "but our meeting today is a miracle to me."

"To me, too. I haven't spoken to anyone in five days."

2

Night had fallen. The stewards had cleared away the folding chairs and the deck loomed long, wide, and deserted. A concert was scheduled for that evening in the salon. Several well-known musicians were aboard ship and the passengers scurried to secure seats. Zosia and I strolled to and fro for a long time in silence. She had already jotted down her address in Boston in my notebook. And I had given her my brother's address in Seagate, Brooklyn. We stopped by the rail and gazed out to sea. Far away, at the horizon, a ship sailed in the opposite direction—from America to Europe. Our ship's horn grunted a greeting. Zosia said, "What an eerie sound these horns produce. It's a good thing fish are mute and probably deaf as well. Otherwise, think of the uproar there'd ensue in the ocean. I myself grow terrified by these deep roars, especially when I am reading. I've resolved on many occasions to read no more Baudelaire. It's true that he's great—in my opinion, the greatest poet of all time. He may be the only one with the courage to tell the human species the unadorned truth. But what good is the truth if you can't live with it? Have you ever read Baudelaire?"

"I don't know French. I've read several of his poems in Yiddish translation. A dreadful translation by someone who was inadequate in both languages. Still, he couldn't manage to destroy Baudelaire altogether."

"I literally learned my French from him. From the day I began reading him I was no longer able nor cared to read any other poetry."

"The same happens to me," I said. "I fall in love with a writer and I remain faithful to him for a long time. In that sense I'm totally monogamous, so to say. My great love was Knut Hamsun. I even translated into Yiddish some of his books."

"You know Norwegian?"

"No, how could I? I did it from German and Polish. A Hebrew translation of *Pan* exists as well."

"Well, this has been a day—or a night—of surprises. Several passengers had tried talking to me, but I have no patience for all this chatter about the weather and whether the food aboard ship is good or bad. Usually when I encounter someone carrying a book, I become interested, but the few people who did were all reading trash. I don't know if you've noticed, but there is a large group of German Jews on board and they all carry cameras and teach-yourself English textbooks. Their pockets bulge with maps of America or New York. I know no German, but if you know Yiddish, you can understand what they're saying. All they talk about is business. It's somehow hard for me to grasp how people escaping from Hitler can be so practical, so well informed, so resolute. I often tell myself that Jews are my brothers and sisters. The fact that my father has a job with the missionaries hasn't altered my genetic cells. I've resolved that in America I will be to myself and to others that which I really am—a Jewish daughter. But somehow I cannot understand these sisters and brothers of mine. They are terribly alien to me. You will probably think that I sound like some self-hating Jew, and you'd be right too."

"No. I won't think that."

"What will you think?"

"I'll think that since you love Baudelaire, you cannot love such optimists as Jews are."

"True, true. But one must love them."

"They don't seek our love. They have wives, children, friends. Baudelaire's every line is an ode to death, but these Jews want to live, to bring forth new generations. If one decides to live, one cannot spit at life all the time as Baudelaire did."

"Oh, you are right. I wander about this ship and I ask

myself, 'Where am I going? To whom? To what?' I am neither a Christian nor a Jew. And why should I suddenly become an American? I tell myself that my goal is to rescue my parents from the Nazis, yet how will I ever manage this? My parents have one desire—that I should marry. In this aspect, they are totally Jewish. They want to enjoy some satisfaction from me. But somehow I'm in no mood to grant them this satisfaction. We've only just met and here I am telling you things I've never told another soul. You'll surely think I'm a total extrovert when in fact I'm just the opposite."

"I know that too."

"How? I've been close-mouthed from childhood. All those who tried to get close to me in my later years complained that I closed up like a mimosa. I had a friend, a young professor, and that's what he called me. But enough about myself. Why should you be so dejected? You're going to your brother and he undoubtedly has connections in all the Yiddish circles. You didn't cut yourself off from your roots. I'm convinced that you have talent. Don't ask me how I know this. You'll be happy in America, as much as a person of your kind can be."

"Happy? I surely lack this kind of aptitude."

"Come, let's see what's happening with the concert."

We went below. The salon where the concert was being held was jammed. Many passengers stood alongside the walls. A crowd had gathered around the open door. Those who occupied seats at tables all had drinks before them. The performance consisted of an excerpt from some opera. From time to time, a flashbulb flared. There had been a time when I envied those who took part in such recreations. I regretted the fact that I couldn't dance. But this urge had evaporated within me. There reposed within me an ascetic who reminded me constantly of death and that others suffered in hospitals, in prisons, or were tortured by various political sadists. Only a few years ago millions of Russian peasants had starved to death just because Stalin decided to establish collectives. I could never forget the cruelties perpetrated upon God's creatures in slaughterhouses, on hunts, and in various scientific laboratories.

Zosia asked, "Do you want to stay here? I don't have the patience for it."

"No, no. Definitely not."

"May I ask what you would like to do?"

"I've told you about my dark cabin. I'd like to go there. Do me a favor and come with me. That waiter has surely brought my supper and I can't just let it sit there. I must also alert them to stop bringing me any more meals tomorrow. I don't know to whom I should speak about it. I don't know a word of French."

"Oh, all you need do is inform the steward in the dining room that you're eating at my table. I'll do it tomorrow at breakfast. Come, let's see what the waiter has brought you. I must tell you that Frenchmen don't understand vegetarianism. If you told them you were a cannibal, they'd be less mystified."

Zosia smiled, revealing a mouthful of irregular teeth. It struck me that she didn't look Jewish. She might have been taken for a Frenchwoman or possibly a Spaniard or a Greek. The ship rolled and Zosia occasionally stumbled. Odd, but once again I had forgotten the way to my cabin. We came to a passageway and I was sure that my cabin lay within it, but the numbers on the doors didn't match mine. Had we gone too far below? Or should we go even lower? Zosia asked, "What happened—are you lost?"

"So it would seem."

"Well, the absentminded writer! What's the number of your cabin?"

I told her the number, but I was no longer sure that I wasn't making an error. We now climbed up and down staircases. We turned right here, left there, but my cabin had vanished. There was no one to stop and ask directions since everyone was at the concert.

Zosia said, "Are you sure that's your cabin number? It seems that such a number doesn't exist at all."

"What number did I tell you?"

She repeated the number. No, that wasn't the right one. On the first night of the journey I had resolved to take the cabin key along with me wherever I went, but the key was too big and heavy to carry around and I had not locked the door. Why hadn't I at least written the number down?

Zosia asked, "Are you not by chance a stowaway?"

"Figuratively, yes."

"Well, don't be so perturbed. My father is just like you. Ten times a day he loses his glasses. He comes in and starts to yell, 'Where are my glasses? Where is my fountain pen? Where is my wallet?' Quite often the glasses are sitting right on his nose."

At that moment the correct number came to my mind. Within a minute we were standing before my cabin door. I opened it, lit the lamp, and encountered a fresh surprise. On my table stood a huge fruit salad and a bottle of wine. Either the surly waiter had repented or someone had realized that I was being done a disservice. Or could it be that my resentment toward the waiter was a result of a whole series of hallucinations? Everything was possible. I had compromised myself before Zosia in every sense.

She winked and said, "Quite a nice meal. I would be glad to have such a cabin instead of sharing one with those two ninnies. They stay up til 2 A.M. babbling about some church in the small town to which they belong. Sometimes they both talk at the same time and both say exactly the same things, as if they were identical twins."

I showed Zosia to the chair while I sat down on the bunk. After some hesitation, she sat down on the edge of the chair.

"Is it totally dark here during the day?"

"As dark as a hundred miles beneath the earth. Sometimes I lie here during the day and imagine that I have already departed this world and that this is my grave.

But I have neighbors who shatter the illusion—a French couple. I don't understand what they're saying, but they quarrel constantly. One time it even seemed to me that they were hitting one another. She threw something at him. He threw something back. She cried. Strange, but every nationality cries in a different fashion. Did you ever notice that?"

"No, but I've never had the opportunity. I've been to England twice, and I never heard anyone crying there. I can't even picture an Englishwoman crying. When my father decided that we must become Christians, Mother cried for days and nights at a time. One time Mother came to my bed in the middle of the night and exclaimed, 'You'll soon be a *shiksa!*' I began to wail and wasn't able to stop."

We sat there until 1 A.M. We drank the wine and ate the fruit salad. We had grown so close that I told Zosia about my affairs with Gina, Stefa, Lena, and with my cousin. After a while, I began questioning her and she confessed that she was still a virgin. She hadn't found the opportunity to alter that condition either in Warsaw or in England. There had been many close calls, but nothing had come of any of them. She suffered from a phobia regarding sex, she said. So great was her fear of it that she transferred it to the men too. Her one true great love had been that professor or instructor who had called her Mimosa. He even wanted to marry her but his family demanded she convert to Catholicism.

Zosia said, "To convert twice would have been too much even for such an unbeliever as I."

"Was that the reason you broke up?"

"That and other things. He introduced me to his mother and the disregard was mutual. He himself, Zbygniew, could not make up his mind. We went so far as to spend a whole night in bed, but it never went beyond that."

"So you're a pure virgin?"

"A virgin yes, pure no."

"Someone will do you the favor."

"No, I'll go to my grave this way."

CHAPTER FIVE

I

Thank God, none of my fears and premonitions came true. I wasn't detained on Ellis Island. The Immigration officers didn't make any trouble for me. My brother Joshua and a fellow writer of his, Zygmunt Salkin, a member of the Anglo-Jewish press in America, came to meet me at the ship. After a few formalities I was seated in Salkin's car.

I wanted to carry my valises but Zygmunt Salkin snatched them out of my hands. I had heard of him back in Warsaw. When my brother visited America following the publication in the *Forward* of his novel *Yoshe Kalb,* Zygmunt Salkin escorted him around New York, presented him to a number of American writers, theater people, editors, publishers, and translators. Salkin himself had translated several works from Yiddish into English.

He and Joshua were the same age, nearly forty, but Salkin appeared much younger. In the nearly two years we had been apart, my brother seemed to have aged. The hair surrounding his bald skull had grown nearly gray. Zygmunt Salkin had a head of curly brown hair. He wore a blue suit with red stripes, a shirt of a similar pattern, and a gaudy tie. He spoke an old-home Yiddish without the English words employed by the American tourists I had encountered in Warsaw. Still, I could determine from his speech that he had already spent many years in the land of Columbus.

He had heard about me through my brother. He had read in the magazine *Globus* the serialization of my novel, as well as several of my stories in the *Forward,* and he began to call me by my first name.

Before driving my brother and me to Seagate, where Joshua was now living, he wanted to show me New York. In the two hours that he drove us around I saw much—the avenues with the metal bridges, the "els," looming overhead and the electric trains racing, as well as Fifth and Madison avenues, Radio City, Riverside Drive, and later, Wall Street, the streets and markets around the Lower East Side, and finally the ten-story *Forward* building where my brother worked as a staff member. I had forgotten that it was the first of May, but the columns of the *Forward* building were completely draped in red and a large throng stood before the building listening to a speaker.

We crossed the bridge to Brooklyn and a new area of New York revealed itself to me. It was less crowded, had almost no skyscrapers, and resembled more a European city than Manhattan, which impressed me as a giant exhibition of Cubist paintings and theater props. Without realizing it, I registered whatever uniqueness I could see in the houses, the stores, the shops. The people here walked, they did not rush and run. They all wore new and light clothes. Within kosher butcher shops, bones were sawed rather than chopped with cleavers. The stores featured potatoes alongside oranges, radishes next to pineapples. In drugstores, food was served to men and women seated on high stools. Boys holding sticks resembling rolling pins and wearing huge gloves on one hand played ball in the middle of the streets. They bellowed in adult voices. Among shoe, lamp, rug stores and flower shops stood a mortuary. Pallbearers dressed in black carried out a coffin decorated in wreaths and loaded it into a car draped with curtains. The family or whoever came to the funeral did not show on their faces any sign of mourning. They conversed and behaved as if death was an everyday occurrence to them.

We came to Coney Island. To the left, the ocean flashed and flared with a blend of water and fire. To the right, carrousels whirled, youths shot at tin ducks. On rails emerging from a tunnel, then looming straight up into the pale blue sky, boys rode metal horses while girls sitting behind them shrieked. Jazz music throbbed, whistled, screeched. A mechanical man, a robot, laughed hollowly. Before a kind of museum, a black giant cavorted with a midget on each arm. I could feel that some mental catastrophe was taking place here, some mutation for which there was no name in my vocabulary, not even a beginning of a notion. We drove through a gate with a barrier and guarded by a policeman, and it suddenly

grew quiet and pastoral. We pulled up before a house with turrets and a long porch where elderly people sat and warmed themselves in the sun. My brother said, "This is the bastion of Yiddishism. Here, it's decided who is mortal or immortal, who is progressive or reactionary."

I heard someone ask, "So you've brought your brother?"

"Yes, here he is."

"Greetings!"

I got out of the car and a soft and moist hand clasped mine. A tiny man wearing a pair of large sunglasses said, "You don't know me. How could you? But I know you. I read *Globus* faithfully. Thanks is due you for writing the naked truth. The scribblers here try to persuade the reader that the *shtetl* was a paradise full of saints. So comes along someone from the very place and he says 'stuff and nonsense!' They'll excommunicate you here, but don't be alarmed."

"He's just arrived and already he's getting compliments," remarked another individual with a head of milk-white hair and a freshly sunburned round face. "I had to wait twenty years before I heard a kind word in America. The fact is that I'm still waiting . . . cheh, cheh, cheh. . . ."

My brother and Zygmunt Salkin exchanged a few more words with a girl who served someone a cup of tea, then we got in the car and drove for a few seconds and stopped before another house. My brother said, "This is where we live."

I looked up and saw my sister-in-law, Genia, and their son, Yosele. Genia seemed the same but Yosele had grown. Out of habit I started to address him in Polish but it turned out that he had completely forgotten that language. He spoke English now and also knew a little Yiddish.

My brother lived in a house built as a summer residence. It consisted of a bedroom and a huge room which served as a combination living and dining room. There was no kitchen here, only a kitchenette, which opened like a closet. Joshua told me that he planned to spend only the summer here. The furniture belonged to the landlord, who was the brother of a well-known Yiddish critic. The bathroom was shared with another tenant, a writer too. Genia reminded me to latch the door to the other apartment when I used the bathroom, and to unlatch it when I was through. Fortunately, the neighbor was an elderly bachelor who was away most of the day, she observed.

My brother had rented a room in the same house for me. The death of Yasha, the older boy, had driven the family into a depression and I saw that the passage of time hadn't diminished it. My sister-in-law tried to cheer up in my presence. She asked me for all kinds of details about Warsaw, the literary crowd there, and about me

personally, but her eyes reflected that blend of grief and fear I had seen there back in Warsaw. She barely restrained herself from crying. My brother paced to and fro and praised America. He told me that he had grown enamored of this country, its freedom, its tolerance, its treatment of Jews and other minorities. Here in the United States he had written a new novel, *The Brothers Ashkenazi,* which had appeared in Yiddish and which was now being translated into English.

Zygmunt Salkin had said good-bye to us and had gone back to Manhattan. Before leaving, he told me that he had plans for me. He mentioned casually that I was dressed too warmly for an American summer. Here, there was practically no spring. The moment winter was over, the heat waves began. No one here wore a stiff collar, such a heavy suit as mine, or a black hat. The vest had gone out of style too. America aspired to lightness in every aspect of behavior. I watched him get into his car. He turned the steering wheel and, in a second, he was gone.

My sister-in-law confirmed Salkin's words. Here, the climate was different and so the life-style—eating, dressing, the attitude toward people. Only the Yiddish writers remained the same as in the old country, but their children all spoke English and were full-fledged Americans.

After a while, my brother took me to my room. It was small, with a sofa that could be transformed into a bed at night, a table, two chairs, and a glass-doored cabinet which my brother had stacked with a number of Yiddish books for me. On a rod running the length of a wall hung hangers for clothes. I wasn't used to removing my jacket during the day but my brother insisted I do so, along with my vest, collar, and tie. He critically considered my wide suspenders and jokingly remarked that I resembled a Western sheriff. He said, "Well, you're in America and one way or another you'll stay here. Your tourist visa will be extended for a year or two and I'll do everything possible to keep you from going back. All hell will break out over there. Should you meet a girl who was born here, and should she appeal to you enough to marry, you'll get a permanent visa on the spot."

I blushed. In the presence of my brother, I had remained a shy little boy.

2

My sister-in-law didn't prepare dinner that night. We ate with our landlord and his family. Although he was the brother of a well-known critic and fervent Yiddishist, his children knew no Yiddish. They sat at the table in silence. When they did speak, it was in a murmur. Our presence at the table apparently disturbed them. They might have been leftists and heard that my brother was an anti-Communist. My brother remarked that Jewish youths in Poland had already grown disenchanted with communism, or at least with Stalinism, but here in

America the young were communistically inclined. What did they know of the evils perpetrated in Stalin's paradise? True, if one of them did go to Russia to help build socialism, he was never heard from again, but this was interpreted by those remaining as meaning that he no longer wished any contact with the capitalist society, not even with his old comrades.

My brother said, "They are all hypnotized. I never knew that a few pamphlets and magazines filled with banalities could possess such a strength. On the other hand, if such a scoundrel as Hitler could hypnotize Germany, why shouldn't Stalin be able to fool the world?"

We finished our meal quickly. My brother told me that he still had some work to do on his novel that day. Yosele attended school and he had homework to do. My brother confided to me that Yosele suffered from nervous anxiety. He was afraid to remain alone in the house, even by day. He hadn't forgotten his elder brother. My sister-in-law wasn't able to sleep nights.

I said good night and went to my room. I didn't have to use my brother's bathroom since there was a bathroom with a shower and a tub in the hall. In my room I lit the ceiling lamp, took a Yiddish book out of the cabinet, and tried to read, but I quickly became bored. I glanced into my notebook, where I had jotted down various themes for short stories. None of them appealed to me at the moment. A deep gloom came over me, the likes of which I had never before experienced, or at least I thought so. I gazed out the window. Seagate lay in suburban darkness. It had grown cool toward evening. The roar of the ocean sounded like wheels rolling over stone. A bell tolled slowly and monotonously. Whirls of fog spun in the air. For all my difficulties in Warsaw, I had been self-sufficient there, an adult, connected with women. I could always drop in at the Writers' Club if I had nothing better to do. I knew that this sort of club didn't exist here. I had heard of the Cafe Royal, which was frequented by Yiddish literati, but my sister-in-law had informed me that to get there I had to first take a bus to Surf Avenue, a streetcar to Stillwell Avenue, then travel for an hour on the subway, and after getting off in Manhattan, still have to walk a good distance to Second Avenue. Besides, I knew no one there. And what of the trip back? I lay down on the sofa, not knowing what to do with myself. I didn't have the slightest desire to write. I had read accounts of the difficulties encountered by immigrants to America, but these hadn't been lone individuals. Whatever they went through they shared with fellow countrymen, relatives, co-workers in sweatshops, boarders with whom they shared a corner of a room or even a bed. Some arrived with wives and children at their sides. But I had managed it so that I would arrive all alone in a dark cabin, and stay with a family of strict individualists who were as isolated and withdrawn as I myself. And what would I do here? Since the urge to write had deserted me, I had to find some other occupation. However, as a tourist, I lacked the right to work. How was it I hadn't foreseen all this? What had happened to my logic, my imagination?

I had opened the window. The air here was damp, oppressive. I wanted to go for a walk, but how would I find the house again? As far as I could see, it had no street number. I didn't know a word of English. I would get lost and be forced to stay out all night. I was liable to be arrested and charged with being a vagrant (I had read in translation Jack London's stories about tramps). Still, I couldn't just sit here. To cover any contingency, I took along my Polish passport with the American visa. True, I could have stopped by my brother's apartment and obtained such information as the address of the house, but I knew that he was working on his novel. Genia might have gone to sleep.

After a long hesitation I decided to take a walk. Outside, I made a mental note—there were two white columns at the front of the porch. No other house on the street had them. I walked slowly and each time glanced back at the house with the two columns. I had read accounts of spies, revolutionaries, of such explorers as Sven Hedin, Amundsen, and Captain Scott who wandered over deserts, ice fields, and jungles. They were able to determine their locations under the most bewildering conditions, and here I trembled about getting lost in such a tiny community as Seagate. I had walked, not knowing where, and had come to the beach. This wasn't the open sea, since I could see lights flashing on some faraway shore. A lighthouse cast its beams. The foamy waves mounted and crashed against a stony breakwater. The beach wasn't sandy but overgrown with weeds. Chunks of driftwood and vegetation spewed forth by the sea lay scattered about. It smelled here of dead fish and something else marinelike and unfamiliar. I trod on seashells. I picked one up and studied it—the armor of a creature that had been born in the sea and apparently had died there as well, or had been eaten despite its protection.

I looked for a star in the sky but the glow of New York City, or maybe Coney Island, made the sky opaque and reddish. Not far from the shore, a small boat tugged three dark barges. I had just come from eight days at sea, yet the ocean seemed as alien as if I were seeing it for the first time. I inhaled the cool air. Maybe simply walk into the sea and put an end to the whole mess? After long brooding, I headed back. It was my impression that I had been following a straight path, but I had already walked quite a distance back and the house with the white columns was nowhere in sight. I reached the fence that separated Seagate from Coney Island and spotted the policeman guarding the gate.

I turned around to go back. Someone had once advised me to always carry a compass. I'm the worst fumbler and clod under the sun, I scolded myself. A compass wouldn't have helped me. It would only have confused me further. Possible Freud might have unraveled my mystery. I suffered from a kind of disorientation complex. Could this have anything to do with my repressed sexual urges? The fact is that it was inherited. My mother and father lived for years in Warsaw and they never knew the way to Nalewki Street. When Father journeyed to visit the Radzymin Rabbi on the holidays, Joshua had to escort him to the streetcar and later buy his ticket and seat him in the narrow-gauge railroad running to Radzymin. In our house there hovered the fear of the outside, of gentile languages, of trains, cars, of the hustle and bustle of business, even of Jews who had dealings with lawyers, the police, could speak Russian or even Polish. I had gone away from God, but not from my heritage.

What now? I asked myself. I felt like laughing at my own helplessness. I turned back and saw the house with the two white columns. It had materialized as if from the ground. I came up to the house and spotted my brother outlined within the illuminated window. He sat at a narrow table with a pen in one hand, a manuscript in the other. I had never thought about my brother's appearance, but that evening I considered him for the first time with curiosity, as if I weren't his brother but some stranger. Everyone I had encountered in Seagate this day had been sunburned, but his long face was pale. He read not only with his eyes but mouthed the words as he went along. From time to time, he arched his brows with an expression that seemed to ask, How could I have written

this? and promptly commenced to make long strokes with the pen and cross out. The beginning of a smile formed upon his thin lips. He raised the lids of his big blue eyes and cast a questioning glance outside, as if suspecting that someone in the street was observing him. I felt as if I could read his mind: It's all vanity, this whole business of writing, but since one does it, one must do it right.

A renewed surge of love for my brother coursed through me. He was not only my brother but my father and master as well. I could never address him first. I always had to wait for him to make the first overture. I went back to my room and lay down on the sofa. I did not put on the light. I lay there in the darkness. I was still young, not yet thirty, but I was overcome by a fatigue that most probably comes with old age. I had cut off whatever roots I had in Poland yet I knew that I would remain a stranger here to my last day. I tried to imagine myself in Hitler's Dachau, or in a labor camp in Siberia. Nothing was left for me in the future. All I could think about was the past. My mind returned to Warsaw, to Swider, to Stefa's apartment on Niecala Street, to Esther's furnished room on Swietojerska. I again had to tell myself that I was a corpse.

3

My brother apparently sensed my melancholy since he did things for me with a particular energy. He and Zygmunt Salkin took me to Manhattan and forced me to exchange my heavy black Warsaw suit for a light American summer outfit. I also had to discard my stiff collar for a soft-collared shirt. Without even consulting me, Joshua arranged for the *Forward* to provide me with work and possibly publish a novel of mine as well. He took me along to the Cafe Royal downtown on Second Avenue and introduced me to writers, to theater people. But my shyness returned with all its indignities. I blushed when he introduced me to women. I lost my tongue when men spoke to me and asked me questions. The actresses all claimed that my brother and I were as alike as two drops of water. They joked with me, tried flirting with me, made the comments of those who have long since shed every inhibition. The writers could hardly bring themselves to believe that I was the one who had written such a diabolical work as *Satan in Goray* and had published in *Globus* biting reviews of the works of famous Yiddish writers in Poland, Russia, and America. My brother fully realized what I was enduring and he tried to help me, but this only exacerbated my embarrassment. I sweated and my heart pounded. A waiter brought me food. I couldn't swallow a bite. A rage filled me against America, against my brother for bringing me here, and against myself and my accursed nature. The enemy reposing within me had scored a smashing victory. In my anxiety I resolved to book a return trip to Poland as quickly as possible and to jump overboard en route there.

I had reverted to boyhood, and those who came up to the table to greet me wondered and shrugged their shoulders. Zygmunt Salkin went off to make a phone call, someone called my brother to another phone, and I was left sitting there alone. The waiter came up and asked, "Why aren't you eating your blintzes? Don't they look good?"

"Thank you. Maybe later."

"When blintzes get cold they turn into knishes," the waiter joked.

Those at the nearby tables who had heard laughed and repeated the joke to others. They wagged their fingers at me. Outside, night had fallen. The lights went on on the marquee over the Yiddish theater across the street. The door to the cafe kept on swinging to and fro. Men and women who apparently weren't part of the literary establishment or the Yiddish theater came in to catch a glimpse of the writers and actors. They kept on entering and leaving. They pointed to those occupying the tables.

Some of the writers here peddled their own books. They wrote dedications on flyleaves and stuck the money uncounted into their breast pockets. A German-speaking tie salesman came in and tried to display his colorful wares and a waiter chased him. A heavyset woman entered. She was bedecked with jewelry, her cheeks thickly smeared with rouge, her eyes heavy with mascara. She teetered as if about to fall. The women applauded her and the men rose to assist her to her seat. I heard mention of a name that struck me as familiar and murmurs of "Just out of the hospital . . . A woman past eighty . . ."

My brother and Zygmunt Salkin returned simultaneously. Joshua glanced at me in reproof. "Why don't you eat? What's the matter with you?"

"Really, I can't."

Salkin said good-bye. He had an appointment. He promised to phone me. After he left, my brother observed, "He has countless appointments. He has a thousand schemes on how to elevate the so-called culture in America, but nothing ever comes of any of them. He has already divorced three wives and is playing around with a woman who will destroy whatever is left of him."

We left and walked up Second Avenue toward Fourteenth Street. Boys dashed about hawking the next day's newspapers in English and Yiddish. Before the Yiddish theaters, crowds had begun to gather. My brother said, "We came to America too late. Even in the nearly two years I've been here, three or four Yiddish theaters have gone under. But there are still hundreds of thousands of Jews who know no other language but Yiddish. They are force-fed on *kitsch,* but that's what they're accustomed to. It's not much better on Broadway. The same mentality prevails there too. Hollywood is one chunk of nonsense, literally an insane asylum. But one talent they all possess—to make money."

We had come to the subway station and my brother

bought a newspaper featuring a picture of Hitler. We rode to Grand Central Station. From there we took a train to Times Square, then transferred to a third train heading downtown to Coney Island. Doors opened and closed on their own. The brick-red linoleum floor of the car was littered with newspapers. All the girls chewed gum. I knew it couldn't be true, but they all looked alike. Little Negroes shined shoes. A blind man entered on his own, waved a white cane, and collected alms in a paper cup. The bare electric bulbs cast a yellowish glare. The fans whirled and whistled over the heads of those clinging to the leather straps. Past the windows raced black boulders, the violated innards of the earth which bore the yoke of New York City. My brother began reading the English newspaper and read it until we came to Stillwell Avenue. Then we took the Surf Avenue trolley. The lights of Coney Island made the sky glow, darkened the sea, dazzled my eyes. The clang and clamor deafened my ears. A drunk was making a speech praising Hitler, cursing the Jews. I heard my brother say, "Try to describe this! There are hundreds of objects here for which there are no words in Yiddish. They may not even have names in English. All life in America keeps constantly changing. How can such a nation create a real literature? Here, books grow out of date overnight just like newspapers. The newspapers print new editions every few hours. I get an occasional urge to write about America, but how can you describe character when everything

around is rootless? Among the immigrants the father speaks one language and the son another. Often, the father himself has already half-forgotten his. There are a few Yiddish writers here who write about America, but they lack flavor. Later on in the summer they'll all come to Nesha's and you'll meet them."

"Who is Nesha?"

"Oh, hasn't Genia introduced you to her yet? She rents rooms to writers in her house. She is one of my most fervent admirers. Yours, too. I gave her *Globus* to read. Whatever happens, you stick to your work. I'll buy you a Yiddish typewriter."

"What for? I can't write on a typewriter."

"You'll learn. Abe Cahan is already an old man, and it's hard for him to read a handwritten text. The linotype operators make fewer errors when they work from typed material. You've got your own room and, for the present, you needn't worry about a thing. Find the right theme. Cahan loves description. He hates commentary. In that aspect, he is on the right path. I often envy scientists. They discover things and aren't completely dependent upon opinions. Well, but it's already too late for me to change and for you, too."

4

No, Genia had not introduced me to Nesha yet, but one day she did. Nesha's house was just a couple of steps from our house. The writers who were staying there presently would be on the beach after breakfast and no one would disturb us. I didn't have the slightest urge to go there but I couldn't go on thwarting Genia. I surmised that she had already promised Nesha to bring me over, and I couldn't make a liar out of her.

The month of May hadn't yet passed but the heat had already begun. We walked less than five minutes and came to the house with the turrets where we had paused on the first day of my arrival in America. On the lawn stood a woman watering flowers. I saw her from behind— a slim figure, her black hair done up into a chignon. Genia called her name and she turned to face us, holding the watering can. In a second I saw that hers was a classic beauty, but she was no longer young—in her late thirties or maybe already forty. Her eyes were black, her nose straight, her face narrow, with a delicately shaped mouth and a long neck. She wore a white dress and a black apron. I even managed to notice that her legs were straight and her toes showing through the open slippers weren't twisted and gnarled as were those of most of the women of her generation.

She too regarded me for a moment, and before my sister-in-law could manage to introduce me, she said, "I know, I know, your brother-in-law. I am a reader of yours. Your brother gave me that magazine—what's it called?—and I read your novel from beginning to end. My only regret was that it ended so soon."

"Oh, I thank you very much."

"Since she already knows you, there's no sense in introducing you," Genia said. After a while, she added, "This is Nesha."

For some reason, my bashfulness had left me and I asked, "Shortened from Nechama?"

The woman put down her watering can. "Yes, right. My parents lost a child before me and when I was born my father named me Nechama—consolation. It's truly an honor and a pleasure," she continued. "I was told Mr. Salkin brought you here straight from the ship but unfortunately I was in the city that day. Come in, come in."

She led us into a hallway which appeared far too elegant for a boardinghouse. The ceiling was high and carved; the walls were hung with old, gilt-framed paintings; an oriental rug covered the floor; the furniture was of the type occasionally seen in museums.

Nesha said, "You're probably wondering at how richly I live. It's not my house. This house was built by an American millionaire for his mistress some seventy years ago. He was already then an old man and she was still young. In those days, Jews didn't live here. Seagate was a summer resort for American aristocrats. After several years, the millionaire died and his mistress became a recluse. She isolated herself from everything and everybody and lived here for over fifty years. After her death, the house stood empty for a long time. Later, a wealthy doctor bought it but he didn't live long either and a bank took it over. From the bank it went over to the present owner, and soon after, his wife died. I was warned that the house was unlucky, that it was cursed, but I took it over not for myself but as a business venture. But it seems it's not lucky for business either."

Nesha smiled and her face grew momentarily girlish.

Genia said, "Since the Yiddish writers became your tenants, it can't be too lucky."

"Yes, true. My God, I am thrilled to know you. Let's go inside. The writers who are here will soon be coming back from the beach, and when they see you they'll snatch you away. I'll make coffee. I want the pleasure of spending some time with you. What do you say, Genia?"

"Yes, you entertain him. He's always alone. We wanted to take him to the beach and to the cafe but he refuses to go anywhere. He was like this in Warsaw too. Aloof and stubborn. I'd sit here with you for a while but I have an appointment at the dentist. You'll be better off having a chat without me."

"Why do you say that? No."

"We'll see each other later."

Genia cast a glance at me that seemed to say, "Don't be in such a hurry to rush away."

After a while she left and Nesha said, "A noble woman, your sister-in-law. A clever and refined lady. Unfortunately she can't forget the tragic loss of her child. They're here two years already and she still can't get back to herself. As for your brother, you know yourself—a man is stronger, after all. Come."

Nesha led me down a long corridor. It was half dark

and she took my arm. She said, "It must have cost a fortune to build such a house even in those days. But it isn't at all practical. You can't live here in the winter. The heat comes up from the cellar through brass pipes and how that woman could have endured the cold is beyond me. It's a mile to the kitchen. The architect must have been an idiot or a sadist. Practical people won't move in here, even in the summers. They want their comforts, not art. For the writers, it's something of an attraction, but they come late in the summer and either can't pay or won't pay. They stay up till two A.M. with their discussions. If they were real writers, at least, I would forgive them, but . . ."

We entered a room with an open entrance to the kitchen—a huge kitchen with an enormous stove. We sat down at a table and Nesha said, "When that millionaire's mistress died, she apparently left no will and those who took over the house got it along with the library, the paintings, and many other things which were later scattered and stolen. She apparently was interested in ghosts since a large portion of her books deal with this subject. To this day I feel that the house is haunted. Doors open and close by themselves. Sometimes, I hear the stairs creaking. It's always cold here even on the hottest days. Or maybe I only imagine this. Apparently no one was interested in the paintings that were left behind. Bad pictures, even though the frames should be worth something. I've heard that the owner is ready to tear down the house and build a hotel on the site. But why talk about the house? What about you? How do you feel in the new country?"

"Confused."

"That's how we all felt when we first came. Uprooted, as if we had dropped down here from some other planet. That feeling has remained with me to this day. I can't seem to become adjusted. I'm here over twenty years and I'm still torn between America and Russia. In the meantime, Russia has changed too and if I went back, I surely wouldn't recognize it. You hear such terrible stories. Absolutely unbelievable. And that's how the years fly by. As far as I know, you aren't married."

"No."

"I had a husband, but he is gone. I have a son of twelve. He is now in school. An exceptional child, a born scientist. He's won prizes at school and what not. My husband left us nothing. He was an artist, not a businessman, and I had to earn a living for myself and for my child. Someone recommended this house to me but the income from it decreases from season to season. This is my last summer here. I hope you brought some new work along with you. For me, literature isn't merely a way of passing the time but a necessity. If I don't have something good to read, I'm twice as miserable."

5

We drank coffee and nibbled on cake. Nesha questioned me about my life in Warsaw and I gradually told her everything—about Gina, Stefa, Lena, and Esther. I heard her say:

"If someone had told me something like this twenty years ago, I would have considered him promiscuous, but today, for a man of nearly thirty, and a writer besides, to have had four sweethearts is not considered excessive. My husband had six or seven before we got together. He was a highly talented portrait painter and he painted mostly women. American men have no time to sit for portraits. They have to make money so that their wives can have it to squander."

"Yes, true."

"You are a different case altogether. You have no idea where this Lena is? Her parents must know."

"I don't have their address. They wouldn't answer me in any case. Her father is a fervent Chasid. Outside of her, her whole family is fanatically pious."

"Have you heard from Stefa or from your cousin? Actually you couldn't have in such a short time."

"I haven't written them."

"Why not?"

"Somehow, I have a block about writing letters. It's even a burden for me to write to my mother. I make solemn vows to write the very next day, but when tomorrow comes, I forget all about it, or I make myself forget. As soon as I remind myself to write, I become as if paralyzed. This is a kind of madness, or the devil knows what."

"You remind me of my husband. He left parents behind in Europe and he didn't write them either. They would never have heard from him if I didn't write them an occasional letter to which he would add a few words. It was even hard for me to get him to write those few lines. At the same time he assured me that he loved his parents. How can that be explained?"

"Nothing can be explained."

"You speak like him too. Since you have shown me so much trust at our very first meeting—I don't know what I've done to deserve it—I can't hide the truth from you —my husband committed suicide."

"Why? How?"

"Oh, he was one of those people who can't bear life, who can't stand any responsibility. The smallest trifle was for him a burden. He wanted to paint his pictures not portraits, but we had a child and no income. The truth is that he hadn't wanted the child either, but I forced him into it. He had one great desire—to be free —and he gradually arrived at the conclusion that life is nothing but slavery and death is freedom. This is true in a sense, but when freedom comes, the one who is free doesn't know that he is free."

"Maybe he does. If there is such a thing as a soul, it knows."

"If. There is no proof whatsoever that it exists. And what does the liberated soul do? Where does it fly around? Oh, I spent night after night begging Boris—

that was my husband's name—to reveal himself to me or to give me some sign of his existence. But he had vanished forever. I still dream of him at times but I forget the dream the moment I waken and all that remains is renewed sorrow."

"How long is it that he is gone?"

"Nearly four years. There's a Yiddish writer here who believes in spiritualism and things of that sort. He recommended a medium to me and I went to her even though I knew beforehand that it was all a sham. She turned out to be the worst fake I've ever come across. She demanded ten dollars in advance, and when she had the money in her hand, a greeting promptly arrived from my husband. How people can allow themselves to be deceived by such liars is beyond me."

"That's no proof that there is no soul," I said.

"No, but neither is there proof that there *is* a soul."

For a long while neither of us spoke. I looked at her and our eyes met. I heard myself say, "You're a beautiful woman. Men surely run after you."

"Thank you. No, they don't run after me. I'm thirty-eight years old and I have a son. Men don't want to take on responsibilities. Of those who did propose to me, no one appealed to me. After a woman has lived for years with an artist, with all his good and bad characteristics, she can no longer be content with some storekeeper, or insurance agent, or even a dentist. I'm not looking for a husband. Sometimes it seems to me that I'm one of those old-fashioned souls that can love only once. . . . Oh, the phone! Excuse me."

Nesha ran toward the room from which the sound of the telephone came—a muffled ringing. I drank the cold residue of my coffee. That Boris had had courage. He wasn't the coward I was. I won't try anything with her, I resolved. One Gina was enough. She needs someone who would support her and her child, not another potential suicide. . . .

I rose and studied a painting hanging there—mounted hunters and a pack of hounds. Was this an original? A lithograph? What a horrid form of amusement! First they go to church and sing hymns to Jesus, then they chase after some starving fox. Still, great poets wrote odes to hunting, even such a master as Mickiewicz. One could apparently be highly sensitive and utterly callous at the same time. There were undoubtedly poets among the cannibals.

Nesha came back.

"Forgive me. I advertised in the newspaper and people keep on calling me. They arrive in new cars, haggle for hours over every penny, then leave and never come back. They all complain that they lost a fortune in the Wall Street crash. Actually they bargained the very same way before they lost their fortunes. What is man?"

The telephone rang again. "Oh, these idiotic telephones! Please forgive me."

"Of course."

I looked at my wristwatch. A half hour had not yet passed since we were introduced. The writer in me has often pondered about how quickly things happen in stories and how slowly in life. But it isn't always so, I said to myself. Sometimes life is quicker than the quickest description.

CHAPTER SIX

I

I showed my brother the first chapter of my novel and his response was favorable. Abe Cahan, the editor of the *Forward*, had read it too and had published a friendly note about it. I was supposed to get fifty dollars a week as long as the installments were printed—a fantastic amount for someone like me.

The writers who rented rooms from Nesha were already jealous of me, but somehow I knew that there was something wrong with this work. I had marked down in my notebook three characteristics a work of fiction must possess in order to be successful:

1. It must have a precise and a suspenseful plot.

2. The author must feel a passionate urge to write it.

3. He must have the conviction, or at least the illusion, that he is the only one who can handle this particular theme.

But this novel lacked all three of these prerequisites, especially my urge to write it.

As a rule, almost everything I had written had come easy to me. Often, my pen couldn't keep up with what I had to say. But this time, every sentence was difficult. My style was usually clear and concise, but now the pen

seemed, as if of its own volition, to compose long and involved sentences. I had always had an aversion for digres-
sions and flashbacks, but I now resorted to them, amazed
over what I was doing. A strange force within me, a literary dybbuk, was sabotaging my efforts. I tried to overcome my inner enemy, but he outwitted me with his tricks.
The moment I began writing, a sleepiness would come
over me. I even made errors in spelling. I had begun the
novel on the Yiddish typewriter my brother had bought
for me. However, I made so many mistakes that no one
would be able to make out the mess. I had to go back to
my fountain pen, which suddenly started to leak and
leave ugly blots. There was an element of suicide in this
self-sabotage, but what was the source of it? Did I yearn
for Lena? Stefa? Did I miss the Writers' Club? My coming to America has demoted me in a way, thrown me back
to the ordeal of a beginner in writing, in love, in my struggle for independence. I had a taste of what it would be
for someone to be born old and to grow younger with the
years instead of older, diminishing constantly in rank, in
experience, in courage, in wisdom of maturity.

The *Forward* had not yet started to print my novel, although I had already sent along a number of pages to
them, through my brother, and had received an advance.
My picture had been shown in the rotogravure section.
Almost everyone in Seagate was a *Forward* reader, and
when I went out into the street, passers-by stopped me

and congratulated me. Nearly everyone used the same cliché—that I had gotten off "on the right foot in America" while other writers had had to wait years to get their names and pictures in the paper. Some of those who envied me added that I owed it all to my brother. Without his intercession, the *Forward* wouldn't have opened its doors to me. I knew full well how true this was.

I was allegedly a success, but in a short while, following the appearance of the second or third chapter, my downfall would come. I couldn't delay publication of the novel because its date had already been announced. A number of columns had been set in type and I had proofread the galleys. In the works on mental hygiene I had read, it said there was no sin or error that couldn't be righted, but in my case, this was far from being true.

During the first weeks after my arrival in America, I used to stroll the streets of Seagate, but now when I wanted to take a walk I took a side street to the Neptune Avenue gate and walked along that avenue or on Mermaid Avenue. I avoided the boardwalk since that was where the Yiddish writers took their walks. I would walk as far as Brighton Beach or even Sheepshead Bay. Here no one knew me. I already had money in my pocket and I tried eating at my brother's as infrequently as possible since they would never let me pay for anything. Sometimes I devoted long hours to these walks and when I came back after dark I sneaked into my room without seeing my brother and his family. My table was strewn with heaps of papers so high that I no longer knew where I stood with my pagination, which had grown as involved as my writing.

My sister-in-law would knock on my door and ask, "Where do you go off to for days at a time? Where do you eat? I prepare meals for you, they get cold, and I have to throw them out. You're causing us a lot of grief."

"Genia, I can't remain a burden to you and Joshua forever. Now that I am earning money, I want to be independent."

"What's the matter with you? What kind of burden are you? If I prepare something, there's enough for you too. The food in those cafeterias where you eat is junk. Really, you're not behaving right. Even Yosele is asking 'Where is Uncle Isaac? Has he gone back to Poland?' He never sees you."

I promised Genia to eat all my meals with them, but after a few days I again started going to the cafeterias. I was afraid that my brother would ask me how I was progressing with my novel. I neither wanted to deceive him nor could I tell him the truth. He would demand to see what I had written and I knew that he would be shocked. I had but one urge—to hide myself from everyone.

One day as I sat in a cafeteria on Surf Avenue eating lunch, Nesha came in. I had the impulse to leave my plate and flee, but she had already spotted me and she came right over to my table. She wore a green dress and a wide-brimmed straw hat. I rose and greeted her. Her face expressed the joy of an unexpected encounter with someone close. She said, "I stood in front of the cafeteria debating whether or not to go in for a cup of coffee. I drink too much coffee as it is. Well, I never expected to meet you here. You eat here rather than at your brother's?"

"I took a walk and I got hungry. Have a seat. I'll bring you coffee. Something to go with it?"

"No, thanks. Nothing at all. May I smoke?"

"Certainly. I didn't know you smoked."

"Oh, I had stopped already but I started again. Let me get my own coffee."

"No, I'll get it for you."

I went to the counter and brought back two cups of coffee and two pieces of cake. Nesha's eyes filled with laughter. "A true gentleman!" We drank coffee and Nesha tasted the cake. She said, "If I stop smoking, I begin putting on weight immediately. I had never smoked before but I began after what happened to Boris. I even began to drink. But the situation was such that I had to think about paying the rent and getting a piece of bread for my child and myself. That was how I got myself involved in that debacle of a house. All the writers are there now and they often ask about you. 'Why doesn't he show his face?' 'Where is he hiding?' You're probably occupied full-time with your novel. I'm already awaiting the day when it will appear in print. The newspapers are all so void of anything good."

"I'm not sure my novel will appeal to you," I said.

"You're modest. Everything of yours I read in the magazines was interesting."

"Oh, I thank you, but there are no guarantees. Good writers have written bad things."

"I'm sure that it will be good. You're looking somewhat pale. Are you working too hard? You're not at all sunburned. One never sees you on the beach."

"The sun is bad for my skin."

"Redheads have unusually white skin. They burn quickly. As long as you don't overdo it, a little is healthy. Really, you remind me of Boris. I could never persuade him to go to the seashore for the summer. He claimed to prefer the mountains. But when we went one time to the Adirondacks, he sat inside all day drawing. He tried to reach the unreachable in his art. This was his misfortune. Your brother does go bathing, but with no particular pleasure. He walks into the water and just stands there and muses."

"We don't swim."

"The others don't either but they splash around and make noise. They keep on discussing literature, quote this critic, that critic, but what they write themselves seldom has any flavor. Have you heard anything from your friends in Warsaw?"

"Yes, two letters came addressed to the *Forward*."

"What's the situation in Warsaw?"
"It worsens from day to day."

2

We strolled down the boardwalk. Black and white men were pushing rickshaw-like rolling chairs toward us and away from us. I had seen this often before but somehow I could never get used to seeing people harnessed like horses. The day was a hot one and a large crowd overflowed the boardwalk, Surf Avenue, and the beach from Seagate to Brighton Beach. The ocean teemed with bathers and swimmers. A din rose up from the throng, a roar that muffled the sound of the waves. I saw so many faces that they all assumed the same appearance. Nesha spoke to me but I could barely hear what she was saying. Airplanes flew low towing signs advertising suntan lotions, laxatives, and seven-course meals both kosher and non-kosher. An airplane wrote an advertisement in the sky for a beverage. The mass of people flowed by chewing hot dogs with mustard, cotton candy, ice cream that melted from the heat, hot corn, greasy knishes, gulping down from the bottle all sorts of sodas and lemonade. Foreheads were burned, noses peeling, eyes bedazzled by the sun and by the wonders displayed here—two-headed freaks, Siamese twins, a girl with fins and scales. For a dime one could see the guillotine that had beheaded Marie Antoinette, as well as Napoleon's sword, the gun with which President Lincoln was assassinated, a facsimile of the electric chair used by New York State, and models of the murderers who had died in it. A small black-bearded man broke chains and sold bottles of the tonic which had endowed him with the strength to do it. He interspersed broken Hebrew words into his English.

Nesha took my arm. "If we should bump into one of the Yiddish writers, they'll have something to gossip about."

"What can they do to you?"

"Nothing, but we're better off on Mermaid Avenue."

We headed toward Mermaid Avenue, where there was another cafeteria. I proposed to Nesha that we go in for some rice pudding. She smiled and said, "I won't get anything done at home today anyhow."

"What do you have to do?"

"A thousand things. But if you don't get them done, it's all right too. Inanimate objects can't complain."

We ate rice pudding and washed it down with iced coffee. We chatted for so long that I finally revealed to Nesha that I had reached a dead end with my novel. She asked me the reason I didn't seek my brother's assistance and I replied, "I'm ashamed before him. I also know that he's busy with his own work."

"Maybe you'd be better off dictating it?"

"I've never tried this."

"Try it. You can dictate to me. I can type on a Yiddish typewriter. I still have one. For a while, I supported myself this way. The writers gave me their manuscripts to type. That's the reason they know me, and when I took over the house they all rented rooms from me. You won't believe this, but some of them don't even know Yiddish well. English, certainly not. They don't have an inkling of syntax or punctuation. In this aspect, your brother is a rare exception."

"Have you typed for him too?"

"One short piece only. Try it. You won't have to pay me."

"Why would you do this for me?"

"Oh, I don't know. You seem like a lost soul in America. I idolize your brother but I somehow grow tongue-tied when he speaks to me. He is so smart and has such a rare sense of humor. At times it seems to me that he's laughing at the whole female gender, actually at the whole human species. He was once sitting with the writers on my porch and whatever he said evoked laughter. He can mimic people better than all the comedians. Since Boris's death, I've simply forgotten that there is such a thing as laughter. But I couldn't help but laugh that evening. If you like, you can begin dictating even today. The quicker a crisis is brought to a head, the better."

"When the writers see that I'm dictating to you, they will start—"

"They won't see. Half the house is empty. We'll keep

it a secret. I myself would feel embarrassed, especially before your brother and your sister-in-law. The third floor is unoccupied so far and the typewriter won't be heard. I'll try to help you. We can go in through the kitchen. No one uses that entrance. I have typed manuscripts, but no one has ever dictated to me before. I've heard of writers doing this, especially here in America. They even use Dictaphones."

"May I ask if you've ever tried writing yourself?"

"Yes, and I know the feeling of beginning a work and not knowing how to continue. I also know how it feels to come to the realization that the main ingredient required is lacking—talent."

"Maybe we can arrange it that I'll dictate to you and you'll dictate yours to me?"

Nesha flushed. "You come up with such weird notions. You're a writer and I'm an amateur, maybe not even that. No, I've resolved to sooner be a good reader than a bad writer."

We sat without speaking for a while. I studied her and she regarded me in return. Her gaze displayed a mixture of female submissiveness and boldness, maybe even a touch of arrogance, or the self-assuredness of those who follow the dictates of their fate. I liked older women, and the forces that guided the world had sent her to me, I mused. Somewhere within the universe, the destiny of every human being, perhaps even of every creature, is constantly being decided. According to the

Gemara: Every blade of grass has an angel that tells it, "Grow." Apparently the same angel also orders the blade of grass to wither or be eaten by an ox.

"If we are to begin today," I said, "I must go home and get my manuscript."

"Yes, do that. Then come to my kitchen entrance. You remember where that is? The door will be open. And if I'm not there, go right upstairs to the third floor. The number of the room is thirty-six. I'll bring up my type-writer and the paper. You once told me of your romantic conspiracies. Well, this will be a purely literary conspiracy."

And I imagined that she winked at me.

3

We parted not far from the Surf Avenue gate. It wouldn't be good for Nesha or me if we were seen entering together. Most of all, I was eager to avoid my brother. But the moment I crossed the border separating Seagate from Coney Island, I saw him. He stood for a moment contemplating me with a half-mocking, half-reproachful gaze, then said, "Where do you vanish to for days at a time? You got a call from the *Forward*. The proofreader has found a number of errors and contradictions in your work and he demands that you come to the office and straighten out the 'copy.' That's what they call a manuscript here. There were some other calls, too.

Some *landsman* of yours called; actually he is my *landsman* also, although I don't remember him. His name is Max Pulawer. He told me that he is a close friend of yours. He left his phone number. Your book also came. Not bad for a Warsaw edition but full of typographical errors. In Zeitlin's Introduction they printed 'occulist' for 'occultist.' I hope that you're proceeding with your work. You've stopped eating with us altogether. If you're not hungry, let's take a little walk. If you haven't eaten yet, we'll stop at some restaurant."

"I've eaten."

"Where did you eat? Come, I must have a word with you. Zygmunt Salkin has been looking for you. In about two months you'll have to apply for an extension of your visa and he is an expert in such things. If you don't extend your visa in time, that makes you an illegal alien and you can be deported to Poland. These days, it's a matter of life and death."

"Yes, I understand."

"No, you don't understand. What's happened to you? I read the beginning of your novel and it reads well, but I want to see what happens next. They seldom start to publish an unfinished work, but they made an exception in your case. If the subsequent chapters don't come out right, it will be a disappointment to us all. You know this yourself."

"Yes."

"What's the situation? Tell me the truth."

"The truth is that I can't remain here," I blurted out, astounded at my own words.

My brother stopped. "You want to go back to the Nazis? They'll be in Poland any day now."

"Not to the Nazis, but I can't breathe here. I can't even die here."

"One can die anywhere. What is it—did you leave someone behind there? Even if so, make the effort to bring her here rather than go back to perish together. Really, I didn't know you were such a romantic. You always kept secrets from me and I didn't mind, but to go back to Poland now, one would have to be completely mad. What's with your novel?"

"I can't go on with it. It's a physical impossibility."

"Well, that is bad news. I'm the one who's at fault. I had no right to let them begin printing it until you had the whole thing finished. I did it because you told me that this was the way you wrote the book for the *Globus*. Maybe it's not as bad as you think? Perhaps I can help you? How much of it have you got written? Let's go home and you'll give me the manuscript. Sometimes you can improve a thing by just eliminating what's bad."

"It's all bad."

"Let's go home. How many pages approximately have you got done?"

"It's all so tangled you won't be able to make sense out of it."

"I'll make sense out of it. Don't panic. Even if it's all

as bad as you say, they'll print the first chapters as a part of a larger work. It's no calamity. It's happened to me too that I've hit a dry spell, but I always had material ready for at least three months in advance. You had enough time to do the same. Come, we'll see what you have there."

I wanted to tell my brother that I couldn't show him my work, but I didn't dare cross him. We walked silently and we soon entered my room. Seeing the pile of papers on my table, my brother gave me a disdainful look. He had switched on the ceiling light and, with brows arched, began to glance through the papers. He asked, "What kind of numbering is this?"

I didn't answer. He took a long time trying to put my manuscript in order, then gave up and stacked the pages in a pile. He said, "I may read this tonight, and if not, then tomorrow. All literature isn't worth a pinch of snuff anyway. Come in and Genia will give you something to eat. You don't look at all well."

"I'm not hungry."

"Well, it's up to you. God knows I'm only thinking of your well-being."

"I know, I know. But I've lost the bit of talent I had."

"You've lost nothing. It'll all return. And don't even think about going back to Poland. That would be sheer suicide. Good night."

He left. My brother seldom mentioned the word "God." He spoke to me like a father. After a while, I switched off the light and quietly went out. Did it make any sense now to go to Nesha's? I had left her waiting. I could no longer bring myself to dictate to her. I didn't even know where to begin now that my manuscript was taken away. Still, I went on until I came to her kitchen. No one was there. I began climbing the dark and winding staircase to the third floor. On the second floor, someone called my name. It was that quasi-writer and total politician I had met in Paris, the participant in Stalin's Peace Conference, Mr. Kamermacher. He confronted me and asked, "What are you doing here?"

I had stumbled upon the worst gossip in the Yiddish literary family. I heard myself say, "I live here," and I immediately regretted my words.

"Oh? So you have been hiding right here all this time?"

"I just moved in today."

"You don't live with your brother?"

"I took a room here to work in."

"Where is your room?"

"On the third floor."

"Really? Nesha said the third floor is unoccupied."

I didn't answer him and continued up to the third floor. It was dark and I couldn't find number thirty-six. I stood and waited for Nesha to show up. Meeting that fellow traveler here had complicated everything. He would assuredly inform the writers downstairs that I had moved in here and place Nesha in an embarrassing position. They would begin pestering her as to her reasons for keeping this a secret. They were even capable of

coming upstairs to welcome me and encounter me standing here in the dark. I felt around for a light switch on
the wall but I couldn't find one. I tried the doors to the
rooms and none of them was locked. I walked inside one
of them and tapped around for a light switch. Why
hadn't she had the sense to leave a light on in the hallway or in room number thirty-six? I supplied my own
answer: She had been waiting for me there, but after
close to an hour had gone by, and I hadn't appeared, she
had decided that I had changed my mind about the
whole matter.

My eyes began to grow accustomed to the dark. From
somewhere outside issued the reflection of a light and I
saw a bed with only a sheet over the mattress, without
pillow or cover. I left the door open and stretched out on
the bed. If Nesha came, I would hear her footsteps. I
needed a rest after all those mishaps.

I had dozed off and a dream of flying took over—I
didn't fly like a bird but I glided in the air, floating in
twilight and wondering why I didn't attempt this before.
I knew that mountains, forests, rivers, oceans were
stretching out under me, but I had no curiosity to look at
them. There was peace in this dusk. Night was approaching like a cloud, lit up by an otherworldly sunset.
Thank God, it's all over, I said to myself. Someone
touched me and woke me. It took a while before I realized where I was and who it was rousing me.

CHAPTER SEVEN

I

A year had gone by. The novel turned out badly but the editor let it run to its conclusion and I managed to save up a thousand dollars. I had ceased writing fiction and supported myself from a short column that appeared every Sunday under the title "It's Worthwhile Knowing"—"facts" culled from American Magazines: How long would a man's beard be if he lived to seventy and all the hairs he had shaved off during his lifetime were laid end to end? How much did the heaviest specimen of a whale weigh? How large was the vocabulary of a Zulu? I received sixteen dollars per column and this was more than enough for me to pay five dollars per week rent for a furnished room on East Nineteenth Street off Fourth Avenue, and to eat in cafeterias. I even had enough left over to take Nesha to the movies once a week.

My tourist visa had already been extended twice, but when I applied for a third time, it was extended for three more months with the stipulation that this was the last time this would be done. I had some ten weeks in which to obtain a permanent visa or go back to Poland, where Hitler was liable to march in at any time.

I was connected with a lawyer who was supposed to

obtain this visa for me, but the last time I had seen him he had told me frankly that I had nothing to hope for. I was lacking vital documents that the American consul in Toronto would demand—in particular, a certificate of moral character from Poland. I had written Stefa several times and she had made efforts to obtain this for me, but the Polish officials posed difficulties and demanded other documents which I couldn't supply. I had lost my military status booklet and other official papers. I suspected that Stefa wanted me back in Poland. She wrote me long letters frequently, forgetting to mention the certificate that I asked for. My cousin Esther had gone back to her hometown. My former publisher, who had gone bankrupt, had left Warsaw. I wrote to some others, but they didn't answer. Who in Warsaw had the time or the strength to stand in lines and to deal with lazy bureaucrats who merely sought an opportunity to say "no," particularly when the petitioner was a Jew? There remained one solution for me—to marry Nesha. But I had taken a holy vow not to marry on account of a visa, not even if it meant my having to leave America. The reason for my obstinacy regarding this matter is something that isn't clear to me to this day. I knew a few writers who had done just this and I looked upon them as undignified creatures. Perhaps the incident with my certificate to Palestine, years ago, about the time I met Stefa, had left a bad taste in my mouth. I loved Nesha, but I knew that all the Yiddish writers would know that I had married her for the visa.

I was most of all ashamed before my brother. Our parents had raised us to have an aversion toward any kind of sham or swindle. The fact was that this marriage wouldn't have benefited Nesha either. She might have gone through with it to save me from the Nazis, but it would have represented a sacrifice on her part. Besides, I had told her at the very onset of our affair that I didn't believe in the institution of marriage. Nor did she have any desire to give her son a stepfather such as I, a pauper, a bohemian who was ten years younger than she. I knew that she had lost faith in me and in my future as a writer.

It had all become routine. Twice a week she came to me in my room up on the fourth floor and although I forbade her to do this, she often brought me food. She warned me constantly that cafeteria food was liable to make me sick. That summer Nesha hadn't leased the house in Seagate. She had gotten a job as a draper in a woman's underwear factory in downtown New York City and had rented a walk-up apartment in the Bronx. My room consisted of a bed, a small table that wobbled on the rare occasions when I tried to write on it, one lame chair, and a sink with a faucet that constantly dripped brown water. From beneath the cracked linoleum, cockroaches crawled. At night bedbugs emerged from the walls. Once a month the exterminator came, leaving a stench that lingered for a week afterward. The vermin seemed to have acquired immunity to the poison. But the sun shone here in the afternoons and there was a bathroom in the hall where I could take a bath or shower after ten in the morning when the other tenants had gone to work.

I had lost the urge to write but I still kept a notebook in which I jotted down themes for novels, stories, regimens of behavior which I never followed, as well as ideas about God, "the thing in itself," angels, ghosts, and beings on other planets thousands or millions of light-years from the earth. I still hadn't completely abandoned my hopes of uncovering—while awake or dreaming—the secrets of Creation, the purpose of life, the mission of man. I was wasting hours on all kinds of fantasies about megalomaniac achievements. I had a harem of beauties. I possessed a magnetism that no woman could resist. I found the means of freeing mankind from the Hitlers, the Stalins, from all sorts of exploiters and criminals, and gave the Land of Israel back to the Jews. I cured all the sick, extended the life of man and of beast for hundreds of years, and brought the dead back to life.

Going to bed with Nesha was a new experience each time. She would come to me one day a week directly from work, and another day, from her home in the Bronx. True, she often reproached me for having ceased writing, for being lazy and lacking in practical ambition. She often scolded me for neglecting to visit my brother, who had rented a large apartment on Riverside Drive, and for staying away from the Cafe Royal and the writers' gatherings and banquets. A young man my age had no right becoming a hermit. Such conduct could lead to madness. But following her lecture and after we had partaken of the supper she had brought or we had eaten at the Steward Cafeteria on Twenty-third Street, we would begin a session of lovemaking which would last for hours, sometimes until midnight.

This woman evoked powers within me I had never imagined I had before. Apparently I affected her in the same way. We fell upon one another with a hunger that astounded us both. She hadn't lost her husband, she assured me—his spirit had entered my body. He spoke to her out of my mouth, he kissed her out of my lips. I, on the other hand, recognized Gina within her. While Nesha was with me I lost all my worries, all the fears. I called her Gina and she called me Boris. We played with the idea that by some cabalistic combinations of letters we were able to resurrect Boris and Gina for the time of our love game and all four of us indulged together in a mystic orgy where bodies and souls copulated and where sex play and heavenly knowledge became identical. We often vowed to each other to flee to California, to Brazil, to the wilds of British Columbia, and surrender ourselves completely to our passion. Nesha even blurted out that she would leave her son with Boris's relatives. But as our lust gradually subsided, Nesha told me that she would sooner let her eyes be plucked out than part with her Benny, who was named after her late father, Reb Benjamin, a pious Jew, a scholar. I reminded myself that my weeks in America were numbered. If I wouldn't or couldn't marry Nesha, I would be forced to go back to Poland, or try to remain in the United States illegally. But how? And where? And for how long?

Since Nesha had come to me early that day, our love session ended sooner than usual. By ten-thirty, we were already dressed. We walked down in silence the four flights, ashamed of our ridiculous dreams, exhausted from our repetitious raving. Nineteenth Street was dim and deserted. So was Fourth Avenue. Only the cars raced to and fro. I had neglected to deliver my column, "It's Worthwhile Knowing," and I had to go to East Broadway this very night and leave it to be set early the following morning if it was to appear on Sunday. Following my fiasco with the novel, I avoided showing my face to the *Forward* writers and I always dropped off my copy late in the evenings when all the staff members were gone. On the tenth floor, where the typesetting was done, there was a metal box where writers deposited copy that didn't have to first pass through the hands of editors. For some reason the editor of the Sunday edition trusted my Yiddish.

I escorted Nesha to the subway station and on the way we stopped at the Fourteenth Street Cafeteria for a bite to eat and a cup of coffee. This cafeteria did its best business at night. It had become a gathering place for all kinds of leftists—Stalinists, Trotskyites, anarchists, various radicals and social rebels. Here, they discussed the latest issues of *The Daily Worker* and the Yiddish *Frei-heit,* articles in *New Republic* and *The Nation.* By 11 P.M. one could already get items from the next day's breakfast: oatmeal, farina, dry cereals, fried eggs with sausage and potatoes. Many of the patrons were Jews, but there were some gentiles too—men with long hair and beards, elderly socialists, vegetarians, and those who preached their own versions of Christianity or predicted the imminent return of Jesus, who would judge the world prior to its end. Homosexual males and lesbians also made this their meeting place. The harsh glare of the ceiling lights blinded the eyes; the noise of the patrons and the dishes deafened the ears. The air was thick with the smoke of cigarettes. Girls with short hair and in leather jackets *à la* Cheka smoked, sipped black coffee, shouted the latest slogans from Moscow, cursed all the fascists, social demo-crats, Hearst, Leon Blum, Macdonald, Trotsky, Norman Thomas, Abe Cahan, even Roosevelt for allegedly sup-porting the liberals while he actually served Hitler, Franco, and Mussolini.

I had found a table for two in a corner and I brought coffee and cake from the counter for Nesha and cereal and milk for myself. I had gone some thirty-five cents over my budget, but since I was soon to go back to Poland and perish in the hands of the Nazis, what need had I of money? Just as I had been enthusiastic shortly before, so was I seized by depression now. I heard Nesha say, "Don't be so despondent. Much can be done in these weeks. Uncle Sam isn't a murderer, after all. You won't be deported to Poland so quickly."

"It isn't Uncle Sam. It's a single official who decides and does just as he pleases. Someone like that is liable to be a Nazi."

"I'm sure his decision can be appealed. People wander around here illegally for years. They hide, and later they're granted legal status."

"Where could I hide?"

"You're hiding anyhow. Before they decide to come looking for you, and until they find you, war would break out and you'd be granted legal status. Until then, you might meet an American girl who would really please you."

"Don't say that, Nesha, I love you."

"The main thing is that you remain in America. Come, it's getting late and I have to get up for work in the morning."

I went with Nesha to the subway, then took a bus to East Broadway. The night elevator man at the *Forward* already knew me. He always made the same joke—that I dropped off my column like an unmarried mother disposed of a bastard. A single light burned in the composition room on the tenth floor. The linotype machines that clacked away all day stood silent. I often had the feeling that machines were resentful of man because he compelled them to do things that were against their nature. From the tenth floor I walked down a dark flight of steps to the empty editorial office. There was a box for received mail here with separate compartments for the various staff members. My brother had his own box where letters addressed to me were deposited as well.

I found two letters for me and I stuck them in my breast pocket. By the time I went outside, it was half past twelve. I waited for a bus, but after a half hour it still hadn't come. I started walking in the direction of Nineteenth Street. I stopped under a lamppost and tried to make out the source of the letters. I couldn't believe my own eyes—one letter was from Lena in Warsaw and one from Zosia in Boston—one in Yiddish, the other in Polish.

It was too dark on Avenue B to make out the writing, yet I managed to gather from Lena's letter that she had just gotten out of Pawiak Prison. She had given birth to a son while I was still in Warsaw. She had been arrested a few weeks later. Her comrades took care of the child. She demanded that I send an affidavit for her and the child. Her letter consisted of six densely filled pages. Zosia's letter was only one page but I couldn't make out her handwriting by the light of the lamppost. I didn't walk but ran. My legs had grown unusually light. What a joke! Here I was on the verge of being deported from America and Lena demanded an affidavit from *me!* And during the worst crisis of my life I had become, of all things, the father of a child born to a Communist, a grandson of my pious father and the fanatical Reb Solomon Simon. What a combination of events and genes!

I had gone as far as Union Square without finding one restaurant or cafeteria where I could read these letters from the beginning to the end. I reached Nineteenth Street and climbed the four flights to my room. I threw myself on my bed and read. For someone the likes of Lena, her letter sounded almost sentimental. She was now a mother and she loved her child. She had named him after a grandfather and had him circumcised even though she considered this an act of barbarity. She had had to somehow make up with her mother. Because Lena had turned Trotskyite and those who kept the child remained Stalinists, they refused to nurse the child of a traitor to the cause. She feared that they might even harm the baby. One could expect the most terrible things from fanatics of this kind. Lena's letter was full of abuse against Stalin and his henchmen. She praised her mother for having saved the child's life. Reb Solomon Simon would never have allowed such a child into his house and the grandmother was forced to board it with some indigent woman, a retired nursemaid who was already caring for two other children of political prisoners. Lena's mother sold her jewelry and bailed Lena out for the second time.

Zosia wrote that she had written to me at my brother's address in Seagate but the letter had come back. Someone who knew about me had given her the address of the

169

RAPHAEL
SOYER

Forward. She was coming to New York City from Boston now for an indefinite period of time and she gave me an address and telephone number where I could reach her—assuming I still remembered her.

My wristwatch already showed three o'clock but I still wasn't able to fall asleep. I had never wanted to have children, particularly at a time when a holocaust was threatening the Jews, and certainly not with someone like Lena. However, the forces that guide the world always manage to get their way. I tried to convince myself that I felt nothing whatever for this creature, but I pictured it lying in some decrepit room in dirty bed linen, undernourished, weighed down with a heritage from which it could never be free. Lena wrote that he had blue eyes and reddish hair. Thus, he favored my family, not his wild grandfather and uncles with their pitch-black beards and fiery black eyes. I said to myself that already somewhere in his brain were hiding my doubts, my feelings of protest against Creation and the Creator. And would he be a Jew or would Lena raise him to be an enemy of our people? Somewhere within me I begged his forgiveness for bringing him into this mess of a world.

2

I called the hotel and was connected with Zosia. I couldn't invite her to my wretched room and we agreed to meet at the Forty-second Street Cafeteria, near the public library.

She was a half hour late and I was already preparing to leave when, through the window, I saw her coming. She wore a summer suit and a straw hat. She seemed to me taller, fairer, and more elegant than the last time I had seen her aboard ship. She had apparently achieved some success in America. I went out to meet her and escorted her to my table, where I had left a book and a newspaper along with my crumpled hat. I brought coffee for her and for myself. Zosia began questioning me and, as is my nature, I told her everything: about my failed novel, my affair with Nesha, and the fact that I had only two months to stay in America. Zosia said, "Do anything, but don't dare to go back to Poland!"

"What's my alternative?"

"Marry this woman, since this is a mere formality."

"With her, it wouldn't be a mere formality. Let us better speak about you. What's been happening with you in all this time?"

"Oh, a lot and nothing. I received a grant to conclude my studies at Radcliffe. This isn't some minor achievement, mind you. They aren't so generous with grants. I never knew that my father could be so energetic. He established connections with missionaries in Boston as well as in New York. I have often told my father that once I was in New York I would revert to Judaism—if this is possible for an agnostic—but the missionaries in Boston sought me out and tried to block my road back to Jewishness. They invited me to their homes, they began seeking subsidies for me, jobs, even marriage partners. Jews remain forever Jews with their energy and their rage to mind everybody's business. One of them, an elderly man, fell in love with me, or so at least he said, and wanted nothing else but that I become his mistress. He couldn't marry me since he had a wife who suffered from multiple sclerosis and was bedridden or confined to a wheelchair. If we have the time and you'll have the patience, I have not one story for you but a great many. Here in the cafeteria is no place for this. The plain facts are that I have given up my studies. I simply lost my patience for all those exams, the professors, and the girls with whom I shared the house. I had seriously considered putting an end to the whole tragicomedy when I met an elderly woman, a retired professor who was forced to give up her position at the university because she had lost her sight. She isn't totally blind, but she no longer can read. She couldn't exist on what the university paid her. She has a wealthy brother.

"I'll cut it short. I have become her eyes. She taught psychology at the university and also gave a course in religion. After the trouble started with her eyes, she got involved in psychic research. Actually, she dabbled in psychic research even before. She reads—that is to say, I read to her—almost all the literature on this subject, and although I'm far, far from convinced about all those miracles these books and she talk about, this is much more interesting than the religion that I studied in Poland and here as well. At least it has to do with the present, not with wonders that occurred in Palestine two thousand years ago. Even if all those visions or revelations of theirs are inventions, they are at least interesting from a purely psychological standpoint. The professor herself is a strange blend of intelligence, a critical mind, plus fanaticism and credulity that border on madness. I must mention that I have witnessed things at her home and with herself that couldn't be explained. She literally reads my mind. I had never told her of my Jewish extraction, but one day she told me that I had been born a Jew and that I must return to my Jewish roots."

"She probably opened a letter from your parents."

"She doesn't open my letters and my parents have never written to me about my Jewishness. Besides, I just told you she's blind. Do me a favor and let's get out of this cafeteria. It's so noisy in here I can barely hear you. I noticed a park near the library."

We went outside and found an empty bench in the park. Zosia said, "Here, I can breathe. Yes, about my Jewishness. At that woman's house I had time to think things over. I ate there, slept there, I learned to cook, and for the first time in my life I seem to have enjoyed the taste of rest. The problem is—what is Jewishness? Of what would my Jewishness consist? I thought that you would be able to tell me, but you are here, not in

Boston, and you have your work. Some two months ago I happened to read in the paper about a lecture in a synagogue. It was announced that a guest from New York would speak on the subject 'What Does the Jew Want?' and I decided to go hear what he had to say. It just so happened that it rained all that day and it poured in the evening. My professor had gone away to her brother's—he has a house in Lenox—and I took the bus to the synagogue. I got there soaking wet and found exactly five people. Who goes to hear a lecture in such a storm? After a while, they left too. My impression was that the speaker was a rabbi. Actually, he had only called himself by that title. I soon learned that he was a businessman and quite wealthy. The money from the admissions was supposed to go to the synagogue. He seemed to me younger, yet he turned out to be a man in his late fifties. I don't want to overburden you with my problems. It's because of this speaker that I am now in New York."

"What is it—a love affair?"

"Oh, I don't know myself what to call it. We were together until late that evening. He took me to a restaurant and he spoke to me for hours. I had come, so to speak, to pour my heart out to him, although it ended with him pouring his heart out to me. He told me his whole life story. I forgot the main thing—he knows your brother and he knows about you, too. He reads that newspaper for which you two write, and he had met you in Warsaw in that club for writers."

"What's his name?"

"Reuben Mecheles."

"I've never heard of him."

"He knows all the rabbis, all the writers. He even knew my father. He told me that he received your book in the mail. They send him all the works in Yiddish from Warsaw. He married a rich woman here in America, but he is separated from her. They were incompatible, she was too bourgeois for him. I was interested in him for a short while, but such is my nature apparently that I get over my infatuations quickly. I'm afraid that I wasn't created for love even though I'm always enamored of some ideal. The thing that I want to tell you is so complicated that it appears even to me a fantasy, but I've convinced myself that it's true. He is involved with some sect—or how shall I describe it? The leader of the sect is a young man from Egypt, a cabalist who presents himself as no less than having had God appear before him and dictate a new Bible to him, one that is four or five times longer than the Old Testament. It isn't exactly clear to me how that so-called prophet is also connected with some people in New York, not only among Jews but among some Christians as well. They even write about him in the newspapers. Mr. Mecheles assured me that he, I mean Mr. Mecheles, is terribly in love with me and that the leader of his sect wrote him of me long before I ever came to hear his lecture! He says that I look exactly the way he described me. Mr. Mecheles wants me to marry him after he has divorced his wife, but she demands a large settlement and a huge alimony. It just so happened that my lady professor went to spend six weeks of this summer with her brother in Lenox and she granted me leave. Mr. Mecheles sent me a train ticket from Boston to New York and he settled me here in a hotel. The leader of his sect will be arriving in New York any day now. Mecheles wants us to marry according to the law in the new Bible. I tell you beforehand that I won't do it. First of all, I'm not anxious to marry him. And secondly, I don't want to do anything that's against the American law. The whole thing is crazy from beginning to end, but I've already met so many madmen that I'm beginning to think that lunatics are the majority and the so-called normal people a small minority. What do you say to this?"

"Yes, man is mad, and from the ten measures of madness that God sent down on earth, nine measures were received by the modern Jew."

"Yes, yes, right! Right! Why am I drawn to such people? I'm beginning to suspect that I'm crazier than they are."

"In your case it's circumstances."

"You're trying to be nice. I shouldn't say this, but I'll tell it to you anyway. I might not have come to New York, but I wanted to see you. Mr. Mecheles isn't my kind of person. He is an optimist and an extreme extrovert. He must constantly be with people, and in the brief time that we've known each other he has introduced me to so many so-called friends that I'm dizzy from them all. I don't think he really believes in that prophet from Egypt, but he constantly seeks ways to avoid being alone. Even if I did love him, I still couldn't be with him."

For a long while we were both silent. Over the din of New York I could hear the chirping of birds. From time to time, a cool breeze blew. I bowed my head and gazed down at a worm crawling on a newspaper someone had discarded beside the bench. The tiny creature crawled forward, backward, in zigzag fashion. Then it stopped. Was it hungry? Thirsty? Did it want to be free of the paper surface and go back to the grass where it had been born? Or did it feel no desire, no need, no suffering, no joy? I would have liked to do something for this lost particle of life, but I knew that whatever I attempted in its behalf would only kill it.

As if Zosia had read my mind, she asked, "Are you still a vegetarian?"

"Of course."

I wanted to point out the speck of life to her, but it had vanished.

3

A few days had passed. Zosia had promised to call but I hadn't heard from her. One night as I groped in the mail compartment on the ninth floor of the *Forward*, I found there a letter from Warsaw and an unstamped en-

velope that someone had left me. I went down with the
elevator, and in the half minute that it took to get from
the ninth floor to the lobby, I managed to note that Stefa
had sent me the document I had requested of her so
many times and that the unstamped letter was from the
managing editor of the *Forward*. My brother had told
him that Washington had declined to extend my visa beyond three months, and this noble man had written to
say that he had found a lawyer for me who specialized in
helping immigrants. He gave me the man's name, address, and phone number. For all my heresy, I considered both these events acts of Providence. The document
confirmed that I had committed no crimes in Poland.
Stefa's letter was long and I read it carefully only after I
had gotten home. One half of the eight-page letter described in detail the troubles she had encountered in obtaining this document. The red tape and the laziness of
the officials was worse than ever. The other half concerned the situation in Poland and her, Stefa's, plans for
the future. Her husband, Leon Treitler, had finally decided to liquidate all his holdings and to go to England
or maybe to America, if he could obtain a visa. Of
course, Stefa would not leave without her little daughter,
Franka. The German woman in Danzig who was raising
the girl had grown old and sick and she no longer had
the strength to devote herself to the child. Besides, if her
neighbors ever learned that the child was Jewish and if
Hitler invaded Danzig, she could be severely punished.
The child was now with Stefa in Warsaw and learning

Polish, although she wouldn't be in need of this language soon. Of course, she was taking lessons in English. There was a photograph of Leon Treitler with Stefa and the little girl and a few words from Leon in Yiddish with hints about our uncommon friendship.

The next day I went to see the lawyer, a Mr. Lemkin. I brought along all the documents that I possessed. The managing editor had already spoken to him about my problems on the telephone. Lemkin was tall, blond, and youthful. His entire presence exuded the competence and energy of those for whom life with all its troubles and miseries is nothing but the kind of a challenge one encounters in solving some easy crossword puzzle. He received me standing up, eating an apple. He took one glance at my documents and said, "It's not enough, but we'll proceed with what we have."

I witnessed something that astounded me, the frightened Polish Jew. He picked up the telephone and asked to be connected with the American consul in Toronto or perhaps with one of his aides. He called him by his first name and told him about me and my documents. I would never have believed speed like this possible. My previous lawyer, an immigrant himself, had delayed everything for weeks and months. He always began his conversation with the words "We're having a problem." But Mr. Lemkin accomplished everything in minutes. In him I had found the very epitome of the American notion that time is money.

The party in Toronto informed him right then and

there that, among other things, I required a bank book to show that I had money in the bank and wouldn't become a public charge. After Mr. Lemkin hung up, he asked a fee of fifteen hundred dollars for obtaining my visa. This was more than I had managed to save up from the novel, but I knew that my brother would help me out. Mr. Lemkin asked for my brother's telephone number; he called him and told him what I required. He demanded a five-hundred-dollar advance and my brother's assurance of the fee that would be coming to him when I returned with the visa. Then he handed me the receiver and my brother told me that he would deposit the money into my account the next day. Then Mr. Lemkin said to me, "You are already as good as an American. However, the Canadian bureaucrats won't grant you permission to enter Canada. Even if such permission could be obtained, it would take too long to get it and in the meantime your right to remain here would expire and complications might ensue."

"What can I do?"

"You'll have to smuggle yourself into Canada."

Although I had a theory that life in general, human life in particular, and Jewish life especially, was one long attempt to muddle through, smuggle oneself past the forces of destruction, the word "smuggle" made my throat dry.

Mr. Lemkin continued, "Don't be so timid. It's all a matter of a few bucks. You'll take the train to Detroit and meet a little man in a hotel lobby. He'll lead you across the bridge into Windsor, which belongs to Canada. Thousands of Americans and Canadians cross this bridge daily and the officials haven't the time for long formalities. The man who will take you across has his connections and his fee is one hundred dollars. When you get to Windsor, you'll take a bus to Toronto. You'll carry no documents on you. You will forward your passport and the other documents to the King Edward Hotel in Toronto by mail. I'll make a reservation for you there for a couple of days because it takes a while to obtain the visa. In case the Canadians should catch you, you mustn't tell that you are a Polish citizen. You can rest easy, this hasn't happened till now to any of my clients. Everything goes smooth as glass."

My throat was now so dry that I could barely speak.

"What happens if I am caught?"

"Why speak of failure? It's entirely superfluous."

"I want to know."

"They'll surely not hang you. In such a case, they'll put you in jail, then try to deport you to wherever you come from. But if you won't say where you are from, they can't very well deport you. In the meantime, we would have learned what had happened to you and would have begun proceedings to free you. Don't think about this for even a minute. The chances of this happening are as slim as of having a meteor fall on your head. If the bureaucrats in Canada weren't what they are, they would grant you the transit visa in a hurry and you'd avoid having to smuggle yourself across. They make difficulties so that the poor immigrants have to break the law and they, the bloodsuckers, can take bribes. I once thought that things in Russia are better, but there you have to steal to keep from starving to death. An uncle of mine came over from there and he told us things that made my hair stand on end. Don't carry any luggage with you to avoid any confrontation with the customs people. Take nothing along, not even a toothbrush. In Toronto, you can buy pajamas or sleep naked, as I do. I'll give you all the addresses. The main thing is not to display any fear when you're crossing the bridge into Windsor. Behave with the assurance of the native. The consul won't keep you there for long. Two or three days. How is your health? A doctor will examine you."

"I hope I'm not sick."

"How about your eyes?"

"Not bad."

"Don't be such a pessimist. Sign this paper."

He handed me a sheet of paper, which I signed without bothering to read it.

4

Everything transpired in a hurry. My brother deposited money in the bank where I had already saved up my thousand dollars. He also gave me money for the fare to Canada and paid the lawyer his advance. But the fear of being arrested at the border didn't leave me. At night I dreamed of being captured, bound, dragged off to jail. Mr. Lemkin's advice to keep silent as to my place of origin went totally against my nature. I knew that if I were arrested I would make a confession complete with all the details.

When Nesha heard that I was on the verge of obtaining a permanent visa, she congratulated me, but I detected a note of disappointment in her voice. Somewhere within, she might have been hoping for a situation in which I would be forced to marry her in order to obtain American citizenship. When I told her of my fear of being arrested at the border, she said half in jest, "If worst comes to worst, I'll come to save you."

In the last few weeks there had evolved between us a coolness that we could neither admit nor deny. The urge we had felt toward one another had left us. Nesha began to mention the fact that she would have to make some sort of change—the work was growing too hard for her and she was neglecting her son. She still loved Boris, but sooner or later she would have to remarry—not in order to provide someone with a visa but to a man who would love her and whom she could possibly love as well. She complained that the late-night visits to my furnished room exhausted her so that all the following day she walked around sleepy and made mistakes in her work. At times during the height of our sexual fantasies she would emit a sigh that seemed to say, Where can all these dreams lead to? This is all fine and good for a thirty-year-old bohemian, but not for a woman of forty and poor to boot.

In the next few days I was supposed to go to Detroit, but when I phoned Mr. Lemkin he told me that my trip would have to be delayed by a week. I was expecting Nesha that evening, and she called to say that our meeting would have to be postponed, and that if I was leaving in the interim, she wished me a pleasant journey. Zosia was still in New York, and although I had resolved that meeting with her was a waste of time, I phoned her and caught her in. She said to me, "I thought you'd be in Toronto already."

These words were a clear indication to me that my stock had fallen with her as well. Nevertheless, she agreed to meet me at the Steward Cafeteria on Twenty-third Street. I could already read English and I bought an afternoon paper. Another paper, a morning edition, had been left on the table. In the works on mental hygiene that I had read in Warsaw, like Payot's *The Education of the Will* and a similar book by Forel, it was written that reading too many newspapers was poison for someone who aimed to achieve some intellectual goal. The authors compared the reading of newspapers to card-playing, smoking, drinking, and other such habits that kill time and offer no benefit. But lately I had come to the conclusion that a writer can learn much from the newspapers, particularly from the so-called yellow press. They were a treasure trove of human idiosyncrasies and quirks. The day-by-day parade of news mocked all the philosophical theories, every effort to seek out a basis for ethics, all sociological and psychological hypotheses. I had not forgotten that, of all the modern philosophers, Schopenhauer was the only one to quote events gleaned from newspapers.

I drank coffee and read. A combination of a slaughterhouse, a bordello, and an insane asylum—that's what the world really was. From time to time I cast a glance at the revolving door. Would Zosia show up? What would I do that evening if she didn't?

She came late and even from a distance I could see that she was distressed. Her hair didn't look properly combed. In the brief time we hadn't seen each other, she had lost weight and her cheeks appeared sunken. I asked her what I could bring her from the counter and she replied, "Absolutely nothing!"

Her tone was stern and expressed the annoyance of one no longer able to control her emotions. Abruptly, she said, "I'm going to be married!"

I didn't answer and we sat silent for a while. Then she said, "I can no longer go back to that woman professor of mine with her spirits and the whole mishmash. Those things, as long as they last, they last, but the moment you tear yourself away from them, they become sheer nonsense. She herself is still to be endured, but the guests who come to her with all their brazen lies are more than I can stand. The books that I read to her are complete fakes. Spirits do exist, but they don't appear to those fakers on command. I had occasion to read Houdini's book and in a sense it opened my eyes. I happened to come across it accidentally in a bookstore on Fourth Avenue that sells books from outdoor bins for a quarter each. Have you read it?"

"Yes, I got it out of the library and I think that he was more of a medium than those he opposed. This man demonstrated things that can't be explained in rational fashion."

"Odd, I have the very same feeling."

"Who are you marrying—Reuben Mecheles?"

"Yes, him."

"Well, congratulations."

"Don't congratulate me yet. I'm not sure that I'm going to go through with it. He suddenly decided to give his wife what she's been demanding and she went off to Reno, Nevada, to get the divorce. He is apparently filthy rich since he is giving her forty thousand dollars plus a three hundred dollar weekly alimony. How he made so much money isn't clear to me. From the way he speaks, you can never tell what he is doing. Apparently, back in 1929, in the Wall Street crash, he bought up stocks for pennies, and those stocks later rose and began paying dividends again. He also owns houses, and paintings by the greatest French masters. He has a huge apartment on

Riverside Drive and all the walls are covered with masterpieces. I shouldn't say this, but I don't love him and I know that I never will. Actually, I have told him this, maybe not as directly, but he knows it himself. He is definitely not my type, but then again, who is? What he sees in me, I don't know. He showers me with compliments but somehow they don't ring true. If I were rich and offered him a huge dowry, I could understand his purposes. But since I am penniless, why would he deceive me? I resolved not to meet with you again. I'm simply ashamed of my lack of character. But when you phoned me, I had to come meet you. You are actually the closest person I have here in America. I could never talk to my father since he was forever shouting and preaching to me and I didn't believe in his religiousness. My mother, on the other hand, can do only one thing—cry. The moment she begins to speak, the tears come pouring out. Weren't you supposed to go to Toronto today or tomorrow?"

"It was postponed for a week."

"What's with your sweetheart? Is she really going to marry someone else?"

I told Zosia the whole situation. Nesha was poor. She had to support a child. She was ten years my senior. She had no strength to go on working. She had actually been the breadwinner even when her husband had been alive. I myself lived off the one weekly column, which the editor was liable to cancel at any time.

"Can't your brother help you?"

"He helps me enough. I can't take a wife and let my brother support her. What's with the prophet from Egypt?" I asked.

A smile formed on Zosia's lips. "The prophet is on Ellis Island. They won't let him into America. Funny, eh?"

CHAPTER EIGHT

I

That night after Zosia had gone home, I was convinced that she would change her mind about the plan we worked out that evening at our table in the cafeteria. The entire matter struck me as nothing more than one of my fantasies with which I killed time instead of thinking about my work. But when I telephoned her the next morning, I detected in her voice that senseless inspiration I often evoked in those who had the misfortune to know me. Besides, the forces that favor adventurers had done me a service. Reuben Mecheles was due to leave for Reno within the next few days to see his wife, who was awaiting her divorce, and Zosia now had the time and the opportunity to accompany me to Canada.

Had Mrs. Mecheles gotten sick, or had the couple decided to enjoy a sort of last honeymoon before parting forever? Zosia did not know, but I knew that anything was possible between a man and a woman. I had observed the very strangest and most incredible occurrences even among those simple couples who had come to my father's courtroom to marry, to divorce, or to settle a dispute. Love turned to hate overnight. Hate flared up again into love. Powerful affection sometimes went hand in hand with shameless betrayal. I often heard critics employ such words as "implausible" and "unrealistic," but I learned that many things that some consider impossible occur daily.

The quiet, reticent Zosia had turned energetic overnight. She was ready to accompany me to Toronto and go on a trip with me to some other Canadian places—"just for the sake of doing something before I expire from boredom," she explained. I had proposed it to her without believing for a moment that she would agree. Only after she consented did I realize how many complications—financial, legal, psychological—this little venture would bring about.

Zosia told me that an immigrant who has first papers requires only permission to leave the country, and she went to a lawyer to help her obtain this permission. She hadn't brought along enough clothes to New York, she told me, and she went shopping for the garments she would need on her journey. The whole thing had to remain a secret not only from my brother but from my lawyer as well. According to his schedule, I was to come back to New York the day after obtaining my visa, but why couldn't I remain in Canada longer? Even if the Canadian police nabbed me for being an illegal entrant, they wouldn't deport me to Poland after my getting the visa, but would send me back to the States.

My urge for conspiracy was, it seemed, even stronger than my cowardice. I became a sudden daredevil. Was I hoping that I would overcome Zosia's fear of sex and transform my trek to Canada into an erotic triumph? Was I looking to take on a new mistress in case Nesha should decide to marry? It was all these things, but chiefly a hunger for suspense. I had made up my mind a long time ago that the creative powers of literature lie not in the forced originality produced by variations of style and word machinations but in the countless situations life keeps creating, especially in the queer complications between man and woman. For the writer, they are potential treasures that could never be exhausted, while all innovations in language soon become clichés.

We had planned everything down to the last detail. We would take the train to Detroit together. There I would meet the guide who would escort me across the bridge to Windsor. Zosia would cross this bridge legally at the same time. Since she had an immigration visa, she was as good as an American citizen. We would then meet at the bus station in Windsor and buy our tickets to Toronto. Zosia was supposed to telephone the King Edward Hotel, where I would be staying, and reserve a room for herself. After I had obtained the visa, we would go on to Montreal. Zosia would tell Reuben Mecheles that during the time he was in Reno, she had to go back to Boston for her clothes, books, and other possessions. The half-blind professor had had her telephone disconnected while she was visiting her brother in Lenox so that Reuben Mecheles couldn't try to contact Zosia. Zosia suspected that he had gone to Reno in an effort for a reconciliation with his wife. She said to me, "For all his slyness, he is a fool, and for all his daring, he is a slave."

Among other things, Zosia told me that Reuben Mecheles' sudden trip to Reno had evoked bitterness among the followers of the Egyptian messiah, for it had been he, Reuben, who had sent the affidavit to the prophet as well as the fare to America. Only such a scatterbrain as Reuben would have abandoned a second Moses on Ellis Island and flown off to a wife who had filed for a divorce from him.

On the night before Zosia and I were to leave for Detroit, I didn't sleep a wink. The day had been a hot one and my furnished room was like a sweatbox. Although the water from the tap wasn't clean, I kept drinking it. I lay in bed naked and the sweat poured from me. My stomach had grown inflated and I had to urinate every few minutes. The same voice within me that had predicted all my other troubles now warned me that my enterprise would end in a dismal failure—jail, deportation, even death. It argued, "It's not too late yet to shake loose of the entire madness." I knew somehow that Zosia was experiencing the very same turmoil. In my imagination, I could hear her toss in her bed, muttering, sighing, seeking some pretext for getting out of the situation. By the time I dozed off, dawn was breaking. I awoke late with an ache in my spine. My mattress was torn and its springs protruded. Zosia and I had agreed to share the expenses equally, but even so, the trip would eat up a huge portion of my little savings. I owed money to the lawyer. I wouldn't dare to dip into the money my brother had deposited into my bank merely for me to be able to show the counsel that I wouldn't become a public charge.

I couldn't take along any luggage, but since Zosia was traveling legally, she had agreed to carry the most necessary things for me.

The train was leaving in the evening but that morning I wanted to stop at Zosia's hotel with my shaving equipment, a sweater, some underwear, as well as my passport. Mr. Lemkin had advised me to mail my passport to the King Edward Hotel, but I considered this too risky. What if it got lost in the mail? Without a passport, one couldn't get a visa. It was much safer for Zosia to carry it for me.

Thank God, the bathroom in the hall was empty—all the neighbors on my floor had gone to work—and I could take a bath without fear of someone pounding on the door or trying to force his way in. I had taken a huge dose of a laxative but my nerves were so taut that even this didn't help. I had forgotten to bring soap to the bathroom, but I found a piece someone had left there. Sitting in the bathtub, I thought that my adventure could be a theme for a story or even a comedy. Who knows? Maybe Casanova and all those other boasters had been just as frightened and befuddled as I was. I dressed, packed the belongings I intended to turn over to Zosia, and went to her hotel on Fifty-seventh Street. What if she announced to me that she had changed her mind? I both wished for it and feared that this would happen. The day was hot and humid. I didn't take the subway but walked. We were supposed to have lunch together at the Fifty-seventh Street cafeteria and later meet at Grand Central Station to buy the train tickets to Detroit. We planned to be there two hours before the train left to allow sufficient time for any eventuality.

I knocked on Zosia's door and it was a long while before she opened it. My imagination promptly began to work. Maybe she had moved out? Maybe she had committed suicide? Maybe she was nothing but a phantom? She opened the door and I saw that her night had been as nerve-racking as mine. She looked pale, sleepy, drawn. Two huge valises stood in the center of the room in addition to a small satchel. I wanted to ask why she was taking along so much luggage but I decided it would be best to keep silent. I saw in her eyes the resentment of someone who has allowed herself to be snared in a trap from which there is no escape. She said, "I'm sorry, but I haven't the room for your things. The valises are filled to bursting."

"Why do you need so many things?"

"Eh? I'm a woman, not a man. I can't go somewhere without clothes. In such hot weather, you have to change your underwear, your dresses, your stockings. And since I am vacating the room at this hotel, I can't leave my things here. They don't want to be held responsible for them."

"Yes, I understand."

2

Everything appeared to go smoothly for the time being. I was anxious lest I run into someone who knew me at Grand Central Station or that it might occur to my brother to see me off, but neither of these events happened. I had been forced to leave my sweater and underwear behind, but Zosia had managed to pack my shaving things in the small satchel and my passport in her bag.

We spent the night sitting up in the coach car. We had rented pillows for a quarter apiece and, since I hadn't slept the night before, I dozed the entire night. The car was half empty and Zosia found a bench on which to stretch out. I slept and worried. In my sleep I heard the conductor announcing the stops. In the novels I had read in my young days, the lovers were one hundred percent monogamous, certain of their love. They suffered only from external obstacles—ambitious parents, a wife or a husband who refused to grant a divorce, social objections or superstitions. They were seldom as poor as I was, burdened with problems of passports, lawyers, precarious jobs, sick nerves. But I had never read about any person whose emotions kept on changing, literally every second. It occurred to me more than once to write about myself as I really was, but I was convinced that the readers, the publishers, and the critics (especially the Yiddish ones) would consider me a pornographer, a contriver, mad.

Mr. Lemkin had written down for me the name of the hotel in Detroit where I was to await a man whom I would address as Mr. Smith. Mr. Smith was to leave a message with the desk clerk giving the time of our meeting. I would not need to rent a room at the Detroit hotel since I would be spending the coming night on the bus from Windsor to Toronto. I was simply to sit in the hotel lobby until Mr. Smith contacted me. But the fact that Zosia was to come along with her two heavy valises and the satchel posed unforeseen difficulties. It would look suspicious to arrive at a hotel with a lady and baggage, then sit for who knows how many hours in the lobby with her and wait for a message from a Mr. Smith. On the other hand, I couldn't afford the luxury of renting a room for merely a few hours. And what about Zosia? Was I to take a double room for Mr. and Mrs. So-and-so? Would Zosia consent to it? And what if the clerk asked for our passports?

I had fallen into a deep sleep before we reached Detroit and Zosia was waking me. She looked sick, faded, disheveled. We got into a taxi and we were taken to a hotel that seemed to me fancy and expensive. Two porters fetched Zosia's luggage and we were led to the desk where new arrivals registered. When the clerk asked me if I wanted a room with a double or twin bed, I heard Zosia say, "We aren't married."

"In that case I'll give you two adjacent rooms," the clerk said gallantly. He gave me a sidelong look and handed another card to Zosia for her to fill out. I was too shocked to remember to ask for the price.

Mr. Lemkin had assured me that Mr. Smith would call me not later than 11 A.M., but it was already 3 P.M. and he had not called. Zosia had gone to sleep in her room and, although I was overcome with fatigue, I could not doze off. These spacious hotel rooms, complete with rugs, tapestried walls, and luxurious furniture, would eat up my budget like locusts. I was afraid to leave the hotel to look for a cafeteria or a cheap coffee shop outside for fear that I would miss the call from Mr. Smith, and the prices for our breakfast and lunch in the hotel restaurant were terribly high. Why didn't Mr. Smith call? Every minute or so I glanced at my wristwatch. Maybe the employees of the hotel were in cahoots with this Mr. Smith and informed him that I brought a female with me? Maybe Mr. Smith called Mr. Lemkin to pass along this information and Mr. Lemkin in turn had informed my brother? Someone like Mr. Smith was even capable of denouncing me to the police.

Zosia and I had realized it would endanger our plan if we were seen together by Mr. Smith and so we decided that she would cross the bridge before Mr. Smith took me there, and she would wait for me at the bus station in Windsor. I was about to fall asleep when the telephone rang. It was Zosia. She was ready to go down and take the cab to the bridge to Windsor. I wanted to carry down her valises and wait with her until she could get a taxi, but Mr. Smith was liable to telephone me any minute. Besides, if both of us were seen carrying valises outside, the hotel employees were liable to suspect that we were running out without paying our bill. It appeared also that she wanted to avoid being seen with someone who was preparing to cross the border illegally, and she had to call for a man to take down her luggage. I stayed in my room and sat down to wait for Mr. Smith. Six came and six-thirty and still he didn't show up. What if he didn't come at all? Since he was a smuggler, it was quite feasible that he had been arrested. A person could also suddenly fall ill or be run over, God forbid. I realized now that I had committed a folly in entrusting my passport to Zosia. I should have followed Mr. Lemkin's instructions exactly, and mailed the passport to the King Edward Hotel in Toronto. Why had I gotten involved with this Zosia in the first place? Of all my lunacies, this was the most dangerous.

The telephone rang and it was Mr. Smith. He said, "Come right down. I am waiting for you in the lobby. I'm wearing a hat with a little brush in it and I'll be holding a copy of the *Saturday Evening Post*. Make it snappy."

I went right out into the corridor and began searching

for the elevator, but it had vanished. I raced up and down the lengthy corridor; there was not a trace of an elevator. It's all my cursed nerves, I told myself. The writer within me observed, Literature hasn't even touched on the fantastic tricks that sick nerves can play on people.

From somewhere, a black maid appeared. I asked her where the elevator was and she shouted something I couldn't understand. I began searching for the stairs, but at that moment a door opened and someone stepped out of the elevator. I quickly raced inside it. How was this possible? Could nerves render someone blind? Did they possess such hypnotic power? And if they did, could this power perhaps be turned into a force that worked miracles?

For some reason, I had pictured Mr. Smith as being tall, but he turned out to be a runt. He winked at me to follow him; however, I hadn't yet checked out. The bill came to over forty dollars. I went outside with Mr. Smith and we walked along. During the whole time, he didn't speak a single word to me. The bridge was crowded with pedestrians. We passed two officials and it seemed to me that Mr. Smith nodded to one of them. They let me pass without a word.

I no longer recall whether the distance to the bus station was long or short. It seems to me that the station was right on the other side of the bridge. The moment we had crossed it, Mr. Smith vanished. I had the anxious premonition that when I got to the bus station Zosia wouldn't be there. And that's how it turned out.

The station was small. If she had gone to the ladies' room, her suitcases would be out here. But there were no suitcases in sight. A catastrophe had occurred. Zosia had my passport. I could no longer return to the States. Nor could I obtain a visa without a passport. According to my calculations, Zosia should have been here more than an hour ago. "Well, this is my finish," I told myself.

I sat down on a bench and everything within me was mute. To forget my troubles momentarily, I began to add up my remaining money. I counted the bills and even my small change several times and each time I came up with a different total.

Each time the door opened, I trembled. I tried to imagine what might have occurred. Had Zosia been detained at the border? Had she changed her mind at the last minute and ordered the driver to take her to the train going back to New York? Had something happened to the cab and she was in a hospital? After much brooding, I decided to take the bus to Toronto. If Zosia lived, it would be easier for her to phone or wire me at the King Edward Hotel than to reach me here at the bus station.

The door opened and several policemen (or maybe these were border guards) entered. Had they come to arrest me? I began to mumble a prayer to the Almighty, assuming He existed, "Father in heaven, help me! Don't let me perish!"

I decided to buy the ticket to Toronto. Even to kill oneself it was easier in a hotel than in a bus station. But would they give me a room there without a passport?

The armed men spoke to the ticket seller. It apparently had nothing to do with me. I walked over and asked for a ticket, but the seller gave me a questioning look and his lips formed something like a smile. The policemen stared at me too and also seemed to be holding back laughter. What had happened to me? Had I addressed the ticket seller in Yiddish instead of English?

I repeated my request for the third time and the ticket seller asked, "Where do you think you are?"

At that moment I realized my error. Instead of asking for a ticket to Toronto I had been asking for a ticket to Windsor. Two of the policemen burst out laughing, but one who was older and apparently of a higher rank kept a solemn face and asked me, "You're from the States, eh?"

"Yes."

"Just come over from Detroit?"

"Yes."

Although Mr. Lemkin had admonished me repeatedly not to give my name in such an instance, I immediately revealed my full name along with my address both in Warsaw and in New York, even though the other hadn't asked for it. I did this, first, because it isn't my way to deny my identity. Second, there was a bit of logic behind this. It would be better for me to be arrested and deported to Poland than to remain in a strange country without papers and with just enough money to last me one week at most. Apparently, I was far from ready for suicide.

The policemen exchanged brief glances, as if mutely consulting on their next move. The ticket seller asked, "Do you want a one-way ticket or a round trip?"

"One-way," I said.

I assumed that the policeman would continue his interrogation and I even considered the fact that it would be a waste of money to buy a ticket if I was to be arrested, but the officials began to discuss other matters among themselves and seemed to have forgotten about me. I paid the fare and was handed my ticket. In a way, I was disappointed that I hadn't been detained on the spot. I was convinced that they would do this later, before I boarded my bus. They surely had to understand that I had crossed the border illegally. I didn't have a piece of luggage with me.

I sat down again, and after a while the policemen left and the station began to fill up with passengers who were apparently bound for Toronto, too. Suddenly, I spotted Zosia. Someone carried in her valises and she handed the man a tip. I stood up and Zosia said to me, "They detained me at the frontier. They suspected me of being a Communist agitator, those idiots."

CHAPTER NINE

I

It was all in the past—the examination by the American consul in Toronto (not unlike the examination by the American consul in Warsaw), Zosia's congratulations, her wishes and kisses. As always when something propitious happens to me, I asked my inner I, my ego, superego, id, or whatever it should be called if I was finally happy. But they kept diplomatically silent. It seemed that I had a great talent for suffering, but no positive achievement could ever satisfy me. What was there to rejoice about? The skeptic in me, the nihilist and protester, quoted the words of Ecclesiastes: "Of laughter I said it is madness and of mirth what doeth it?" I was still a Yiddish writer who hadn't made it, estranged from everything and everybody. I could live neither with God nor without him. I had no faith in the institution of marriage, neither could I stand my bachelor's loneliness.

We had eaten a combination of lunch and supper in a noisy little restaurant and then walked all the way back to the King Edward Hotel. For some reason Zosia kept on stopping at shop windows. I asked her what she was searching for but she didn't give me a clear answer. Her feet must have been hurting because she lingered at windows displaying ladies' shoes. I offered to wait until she got herself a pair of shoes but she assured me that she had comfortable shoes in her luggage. Besides, the stores were closing.

Night had fallen when we finally returned to the hotel. In all the excitement of getting the visa I had almost forgotten that Zosia and I had come here with an unspoken agreement to deliver her from the disgrace of remaining a virgin at an age when other women had husbands or lovers or both. I was anxious to keep my silent promise both for her sake and my own male vanity, but from the very beginning of our journey I was aware that something like an antisexual dybbuk had taken hold of me. A spiteful spirit was telling me that agreements of this kind are not only morally wrong but physiologically precarious as well. Sex, like art, cannot be made to order —at least not in my case. The little desire I had for Zosia that evening when we planned our trip together had vanished almost immediately and I began to feel something akin to hostility for that old maid who was clinging to me like a parasite. What shame, I thought, to have to depend on the little blood and the few nerves that evoke the erection! Unlike the other limbs of the body, the penis has the autonomy to function or not to function according to its ethical and aesthetic likes and dislikes. The cabalists called this organ "the sign of the holy covenant." It bore the name *yesod,* the same as one of the ten spheres of the divine emanation. What I really felt now was a kind of negative erection, if one may use an expression like this. My penis tried to steal into hiding, to become shrunken, to sabotage and punish me for daring to make a decision without its consent, to become a benefactor on its account. The resolver in me had resolved that I owed Zosia nothing. I had to remain completely passive, not take the slightest initiative. Let me imagine, I said to myself, that they actually arrested me in Windsor that late afternoon and that I am in a Canadian prison now.

Both of us were tired from the long walk and we decided to take a rest. Zosia had gone to her room to lie down for half an hour, and I tried to do the same in my room but I could not even doze, let alone sleep. I closed my eyes but they too had become autonomous and opened by themselves. If there is such a thing as Nirvana, let me try it right now, I decided. Zosia must have read my mind. My phone rang and it was she, stuttering and asking, "What became of our plan?"

"What plan?" I asked with a choked voice.

"We were supposed to celebrate."

"Come in and we will celebrate."

"All right, I will dress." And she hung up.

What does she have to dress for? I murmured to myself. Or does she mean undress? I waited what seemed to me a long time and she still did not appear. What is she doing in there? Preparing like a bride? I was impatient for her to come in—not in order to fulfill my self-imposed obligation but to void it once and for all. I could neither lie nor sit and I began to pace back and forth. I

stopped at the window and looked out at the street seven
flights below. How dark the city was! All the stores were
closed. A single man, seemingly drunk, passed by on the
sidewalk. He swayed and gesticulated. I envied this
tramp. No one expected anything of him; he was free to
spend the night as he pleased. I heard a knocking on my
door and I rushed to open it. On the other side of the
threshold stood Zosia in a black nightgown (or was it a
negligee?) and silver slippers. For the first time she wore
a trace of makeup, discreetly applied, her nose powdered,
and a redness in her cheeks which might have been
rouge. She had even changed her hairdo. "Unconditional
surrender," the phrase so often used at the end of World
War II, went through my mind. She smiled, half-fright-
ened, with that naïvete which sometimes shows up in
even the most shrewd woman. They understand as little
about men as men understand them, I thought. She had
armed herself with that weapon which had never yet
conquered anyone. I heard her say, "Today should be a
holiday for us."

"How beautiful you look! Come in."

"A day like this happens once in a lifetime."

This was no longer the same Zosia who admired
Baudelaire for being the only poet and thinker who
could tell the world the full dismal truth, but an old
maid who had decided to lose her virginity at any price.
I sat down on my bed and I offered her the chair nearby.
In one way or another I had to inflate her confidence in
me and in my masculine prowess, and I said, "I don't

think that you made such a fuss when *you* got your visa."

"What? I got mine at a time when I wasn't even sure if I wanted to go to America. I have told you already, I had someone who I thought I could love and who loved me. Leaving for America was actually more my father's plan than mine. What could I have expected to find in America besides extreme loneliness? But you are a writer, you have a brother here, a newspaper that publishes you, a milieu. You will grow."

"No, Zosia, I'm completely alone."

"Today I don't want to hear this. Wait, I have a surprise for you."

"What kind of surprise?"

"This morning I bought a bottle of champagne especially for this occasion. The chambermaid saw me come in with it, and she brought me a bucket with ice. It has already melted but the water is still cold."

"Really, you needn't have done this."

"Can I bring it in?"

"Yes, if you want."

She went out and did not close the door, but left it half open. She dallied longer than would have been necessary to bring the bottle from one room to another in the same corridor. After a long while she came back. I got up to take the bucket from her and my hands trembled so that I almost dropped it. She said, "Where do you get a corkscrew in a place like this?"

I took the bottle out of the bucket and let the water drip back in order not to wet the rug. I could see that it was not corked but sealed with a foil wrapper that could be easily removed. I had barely begun to unwrap the foil when I heard a pop. The stopper sprang off and the wine began to fizz over its neck and my hand. Zosia screamed and ran to the bathroom, coming back with two glasses, while the champagne kept on running over my hand and onto the rug. Perhaps the champagne would help me, flashed through my mind, as I poured one glass for Zosia and one for myself. I clinked my glass to hers and gulped it down like medicine. Usually when I drank an alcoholic beverage, even wine, I had to eat something with it—a cookie, a pretzel, a piece of bread. But this time I wanted to get drunk. It occurred to me that this might have been Zosia's aim in buying this gift—to make me drunk as the daughters did to Lot.

We had emptied the bottle. I was still sitting on the edge of the bed and Zosia on the chair opposite. She crossed her legs and for a split second I saw she was naked under her fancy garment. I was waiting for my drunkenness to ascend from the stomach to the brain, but I felt that the opposite was happening—it descended from my brain to my stomach. I remained tense, sober, attentive to the slightest variation in my moods. I heard Zosia say, "I've read nothing of yours, but for some reason I believe in your talent. The trouble is that what a human being is, no one will ever be able to describe. What is a human being, eh?"

I did not answer. I seemed to have missed the question. For one fraction of a moment my mind remained blank. Then I realized what she had said, and I answered, "A caricature of God, a parody of the spirit, the only entity in Creation which could be called a lie."

2

The master of spite, as I call the special adversary of lovemaking, had had his way. The first half of the night Zosia was willing but I was inhibited. After I gave up all hope and had an hour of sleep, my potency came back as strongly as ever but then Zosia became possessed by the same dybbuk. She pressed her legs together and my bony knees could not separate them. I reproached her contradictory behavior but she said to me, "I can't help it." She informed me that exactly the same thing happened to her on that night when she had tried to give herself to that professor in Warsaw. I had gotten so accustomed to the games of the adversary in me and in those near to me that I stopped being surprised. I had already learned that our genitals, which in the language of the vulgar are synonyms of stupidity and insensitivity, are actually the expression of the human soul, defiant of lechery, the most ardent defenders of true love.

Day was breaking when we both gave up and Zosia went back to her room. In the morning we had breakfast in the dining room of the hotel, trying to make conversation about Hitler, Mussolini, the civil war in Spain. We avoided looking into each other's eyes. It was clear to both of us that our planned journey together was over. Zosia had gotten information about her return to the U.S.A. at the desk. She intended to travel directly from Toronto to Boston and I was to take the train to New York. Both of our trains were leaving in the evening and we had the whole day to ourselves. We checked out from the hotel after lunch, leaving our luggage in the storage room—partners to a disenchantment we could never forget.

I was told that Spodina Avenue was the center of Yiddishism in Toronto, and there we went. I again strolled on Krochmalna Street—the same shabby buildings, the same pushcarts and vendors of half-rotten fruit, the familiar smells of the sewer, soup kitchens, freshly baked bagels, smoke from the chimneys. I imagined that I heard the singsong of cheder boys reciting the Pentateuch and the wailing of women at a funeral. A little rag dealer with a yellow face and a yellow beard was leading a cart harnessed to an emaciated horse with short legs and a long tail. A mixture of resignation and wisdom looked out of its dark eyes, as old and as humble as the never-ending Jewish Exile.

Zosia was saying to me, "Oh, I was determined, and I still am, to return to Jewishness, but of what shall my Jewishness consist? If there is no God and if the Bible is a lie, in what way is a Jew a Jew?"

"He is a Jew by virtue of the fact that he isn't a gentile," I said, just to say something.

"Maybe I should leave everything and go to Palestine?" Zosia asked. She spoke to me, to herself, and mostly in order to show that her mind could be occupied with things other than with our common disgrace. I said, "Unless you were to shave your head, don a bonnet, and marry some yeshiva student from Mea Shearim, all your problems would remain unresolved even in Palestine."

"Oh, I am lost. You are lost, too, but at least you received a Jewish upbringing. You know the Talmud and all the rest. You belong to these Yiddishists whether you want to or not. I am a total stranger here. I'm psychotic to boot. Last night, after I had fallen asleep in my room, I heard my father's voice. He yelled at me so loud that I was afraid you would hear it next door. He seized me by the throat and tried to strangle me. I'm seriously afraid that I will soon be committed to an asylum."

"No, Zosia, our so-called nerves are not madness but a true realization of the many misfortunes which lurk before us and of all the barriers that stand between us and our notions of happiness."

"What? They may lead to insanity. My father had a sister who went insane in her later years. She convinced herself that her husband was trying to poison her. I suspect that my father's conversion was an act of lunacy, too. This thing with Reuben Mecheles is finished. I shouldn't have started up with him in the first place. I'll go back to Boston to my professor and maybe we'll get through the few years left to her and to me. You see already that love and sex aren't for me. Come, let's have a cup of coffee."

Although it was too late for lunch and too early for dinner, the restaurant we entered—a kind of Jewish Polish coffeehouse—was crowded with young men and women. They all conversed—or rather, shouted—in Yiddish. The tables were strewn with Yiddish newspapers and magazines. I heard the names of Jewish writers, poets, and politicians. This place was a Canadian version of the Warsaw Writers' Club. Its patrons engaged in the same kind of conversations one always hears among Yiddishists: Could literature ignore social problems? Could writers retreat to ivory towers and avoid the struggle for justice? I didn't have to listen to their talk—their faces, voices, and intonations told me what each of them was: a Communist, a Left Poalei Zionist, or a Bundist. Hardly anyone here spoke with a Litvak accent. These were boys and girls from Staszow, Lublin, Radom, each one hypnotized by some social cause. I could tell by the way they pronounced certain words from which bank of the Vistula the speaker came, the left or the right. I imagined that even their gestures had unique meanings. Zosia and I found a table and sat down. She said, "Here you are in your element."

"Not really."

It was odd that having crossed the Atlantic and smuggled myself over the border I found myself in a copy of

Yiddish Poland. I told myself that there had been no need to consider suicide when Zosia vanished with my passport. All I would have had to do was come to Spodina Avenue. Here, I could have become a teacher, a writer for the local periodical, or at least a proofreader. The Yiddishists would have hidden me here, provided me with documents, and sooner or later obtained Canadian citizenship for me. One of the girls sitting at these tables and smoking cigarettes would probably have become my wife and, like Lena had long ago, would have tried to persuade me to harness my creative powers to the struggle for a better world.

A waiter came over and I let Zosia order the coffee and the rice pudding for both of us. Somehow, I couldn't bring myself to address this youth in English, nor could I speak to him in Yiddish, since he would start questioning me about who I was, where I came from, and what I was doing in Canada. Some of those sitting at the tables had already cast curious glances at me. My picture had been printed in the rotogravure section of the *Forward* and all the New York newspapers were read here. I had even noticed a Yiddish Warsaw paper on one of the tables. Nor did I care to draw Zosia into a conversation that would be boring to her.

Zosia asked now, "Is it possible to go directly to Boston from here?"

"I believe so. Why not? You have nothing more to do in New York?"

"No, my dear. Absolutely nothing."

"Is your lady professor back home yet?"

"No, but she left me a key."

We grew silent. I reminded myself of my passport, my visa, and the paper affirming my right to return to America and to take out my first papers leading to full citizenship. I stuck my hand inside my breast pocket and tapped both the passport and this paper. I had an urge, for the countless time, to read it over, but I was ashamed before Zosia and of my own weakness. Though it seemed that all my immigration worries were over, some force warned me that a new crisis was looming over me, although I couldn't for the life of me figure out what it might entail.

"What are you searching for?" Zosia asked. "Have you lost something or what?"

I had forgotten to take my hand out of my bosom pocket and I quickly withdrew it as my mouth replied of its own volition, "I have lost a woman with whom I might have been happy."

3

I had persuaded Zosia to go to Boston via New York, telling her that in spite of our sexual defeat I had become attached to her and without her my trip would be lonely and dismal. After a while, she consented. We checked out of the hotel and went by taxi to the railroad station. Evening had fallen. We had already gone through customs, showing the officials our papers, and they had passed us through without any difficulties. I had sneaked like a thief into Canada but I left it like a free man. We had traveled some distance, but I was still not completely at ease. Suddenly, the train stopped and two men who might have been policemen, border guards, or customs men entered the car. All the passengers appeared startled by this unexpected stop, or at least it seemed so to me. Maybe they are looking for me? the coward within me asked. Immediately afterward, I heard my name called. I rose and all the passengers, perplexed and not without pity, gazed at me. I confirmed my identity and one of the officials said, "Come with us."

The frightened Zosia had risen too and she made a gesture as if to indicate that she wanted to accompany me, or perhaps to argue with those who were arresting me, but I shook my head at her to desist. For all of my distress, I enjoyed a measure of satisfaction—my intuition hadn't failed me.

The moment we stepped off, someone signaled the engineer, and the train pulled away. The night was a dark one and all I could see was one lighted house. It was there that I was led. I entered an office where a card hung on the wall. It contained rows of letters, each smaller than the ones above—the eye chart seen in an eye doctor's reception room and, occasionally, in an optical shop.

An elderly man said to me, "The doctor at the consulate expressed some doubt about your eyes. I'll test them again."

As he spoke these words, I began to see spots before my eyes. I glanced at the chart and I could barely distinguish the very top row of letters. Soon even they had grown misted over. The doctor showed me to a chair and asked what I could see on the chart. I strained in an effort to guess at the letters behind the whirls of diffusion, but I knew that I was failing.

Behind my back I heard the doctor's mumbling. From time to time he helped me with a letter. He shone a lighted instrument into my eyes. A lump had formed in my throat and my palate and lips grew dry. Still, I managed to say, "It's not my eyes. I'm nervous."

"Yes, yes, yes. You are a bit nervous."

He tested me again and this time I saw better. He called to someone and the two officers who had arrested me came in. Only now did I notice how tall they were— a pair of giants.

The doctor said, "When is the next train?"

They replied, but I didn't hear what they said. Not only my eyes but my ears too had ceased functioning.

The doctor gave me his hand. "Don't worry. Your eyes are better than mine."

"I thank you, Doctor, I thank you very much."

"Have a good trip."

The two officers led me outside toward the tracks.

They stayed with me for about three quarters of an hour and chatted about horse races, hunting, forest fires, and other things in which gentiles are interested. From time to time they also addressed a few words to me. One of them asked, "How did you get into Canada?"

Somehow, I couldn't bring myself to tell the lie that I had had permission to enter that country. Had I said this, they might have asked to see this permission or ask who had issued it. Then again, I couldn't admit that I had crossed the border illegally. I, therefore, said, "I believe that I had permission."

I had already long since perceived that, when necessary, the brain could function remarkably fast. The officer apparently gathered my insinuation for he dropped the subject. After a while, a train came and the officials put me aboard it. Just like the doctor before them, they offered me their hands and wished me luck in America.

I was fully aware that these officers and the officers in the Windsor bus station could have easily detained me. The law was on their side, not on mine. How would Stalin's NKVD men have behaved in such an instance? Even the officials of democratic Poland didn't display too much consideration in such instances. I had been raised to believe that a man with brass buttons, a badge, an insignia on his cap knew little compassion, particularly when his victim was a Jew. But Americans and Canadians seemed different. Why were they different? Did it bear on the fact that Americans and Canadians were richer? Was it the upbringing? Were Anglo-Saxons by nature more inclined to be understanding of another person's dilemma than Slavs or Germans, for instance? I was by then mature enough not to seek reasons and explanations for the conduct of individuals or even of groups.

The forces worked in such fashion that my return, after I had overcome all dangers and driven off all demons and evil spirits, was completely joyless. The car that I had occupied with Zosia had been new, with plush seats, clean, bright, resembling a second-class coach in Poland or France. The passengers were young and well dressed. It was my impression that many of the couples there were going to the United States on their honeymoons. The coach in which I traveled now was old, and its passengers struck me as just as dowdy and shabby. The panes hadn't been washed in such a long time that I could barely see anything through them, not even the darkness outside. I was left with no choice but to lean my head against the dirty seat and force myself to doze off. I didn't believe in true sleep. I had always considered sleep a sort of make-believe, not only among people but even among animals.

I slept and even dreamed, yet at the same time I thought about Zosia and the troubles she had endured during her few days with me. She was probably ashamed before the other passengers that her companion was the kind of person who had been removed from the train by armed guards.

4

I was back in New York, back in my furnished room on Nineteenth Street. Once again I read my visa in my passport and the card I would present when I took out my first papers, then I put them away in the drawer of my wobbly table. The day was hot. The sun baked my face and I lowered the torn shade over the window. Through its vents and holes, the sunlight painted a mural on the opposite wall, a brilliant network against a background of shadow which shimmered and vibrated as if reflecting the waves of a river.

I had failed in many areas, yet I now found myself on a continent where neither Hitler nor Stalin could threaten me. I had eaten a satisfying meal at the Automat opposite Grand Central Station and I was ready to get some sleep after the restless nights on the train to Detroit, on the bus to Toronto, on the train back to New York, and with Zosia at the King Edward Hotel.

I had called Nesha at the factory from the Automat, and from the way she answered me—curtly, impatiently (she wouldn't even try to arrange a meeting with me)—I gathered that everything between us was over. She congratulated me halfheartedly. I had phoned my brother at his home and at the *Forward,* but there was no one at his home and someone at the *Forward* office shouted, "Not here!" and hung up. My attorney, Mr. Lemkin, wasn't in his office either and his secretary advised me to call the next day since he would be tied up in court all that day. I had fallen asleep, and when I opened my eyes, the solar hieroglyphics on the wall across the window had vanished. My shirt and the pillow beneath my head were wet. Suddenly, I became aware that someone was knocking on my door. It was undoubtedly the exterminator because it couldn't have been Nesha and no one else ever entered my room. Although I needed him to spray since toward evening the roaches began to crawl out from under the cracked linoleum, I decided not to let him in. He always left behind a stench that lingered for days. Nor did I want to begin my first day of American citizenship, or precitizenship, by condoning the poisoning of innocent cockroaches. I called out, "Not today!"

At that moment the door opened and I saw the superintendent of the house, Mr. Pinsky, as well as my brother, Zosia, and a small man in a checkered suit and with a pointed potbelly. He wore a Panama hat and a colorful tie with a pearl stickpin inserted into its broad knot. His shoes were yellow, and although it was blazing hot outside, he wore spats over them. A long cigar stuck out of his mouth. He reminded me of the caricatures of capitalists in Socialist and Communist brochures and the labor union publications. For a while, the three of them stood silent, staring at me, then Mr. Pinsky said, "What did I tell you? I saw him pass with my own two eyes. I'm in this business thirty years already and when I see a face once, I recognize it years later. I can see through my

little window everyone who comes in or goes out. You can't hide from me. I hear the telephone downstairs. Good-bye!"

"Thank you, thank you!" my brother and Zosia called out together.

So deep had been my sleep that it took moments for me to orient myself as to what was happening. I had been convinced that Zosia had gone straight to Boston after she returned by herself to New York. Instead, she had notified my brother that I had been detained at the border. The small man in the Panama hat exclaimed, "So that's him, eh? Yep, that's him. I've seen his picture in the *Forward* rotogravure. The caption read, 'Two brothers and both writers.' My name is Reuben Mecheles. Very, very nice to make your acquaintance!"

"Oh, my God, on account of you I had a wretched night!" Zosia said to me. "Everyone in the car thought they had captured Al Capone and that I was his moll. I explained to them that it had to do with immigration and formalities. I didn't want to disturb your brother, but I decided that under the circumstances somebody had to be notified. I went back to the hotel where I had stayed before. Luckily, my room was still vacant. All I knew was that your brother works at the *Forward*. At first, they wouldn't give me his phone number. But I told them that it was a matter of life and death—"

"Why did they detain you?" my brother asked.

"The doctor at the consulate wanted my eyes retested."

"That's exactly what I thought," Reuben Mecheles piped up. "I'm an old hand at such things. I've helped, and I still help, Jews to come to America. I've brought over my whole family and strangers as well. I'm known at the HIAS. A week doesn't go by that I don't come to them on some matter. I have already sent out perhaps a hundred affidavits. The things we Jews have to do—rather than curse Hitler, which does as much good as giving a corpse an enema—is to bring over all those we can. Not everyone wants to come here. There are such fools who still think Hitler is bluffing. They're afraid to abandon their stores and their Polish zlotys. If Hitler should come to Poland, the zlotys will be worth what the marks were in 1919—toilet paper, if you'll forgive me."

"It's terribly hot in here. Where is the heat coming from?" my brother asked. "Why is the window closed?"

"Let's go down, let's get out of here," Reuben Mecheles said. "I came back from a trip yesterday. I flew back from Reno, Nevada. I don't have the time or the patience for trains. I tried being good to a person who is doing everything possible to destroy me and herself. Suicides are terribly obstinate. I shouldn't say it but I made the same mistake as our allies are making with Hitler. I tried to appease a person who knows war only and nothing else and who considers human goodness as nothing but weakness. If I could write a book about this woman, I would become a multimillionaire overnight. I came back from the trip dead tired and I lay down for a nap. All of a sudden, the phone rings. And who is it? Our good friend, Zosia, and she tells me you've been arrested at the border and that you must be instantly rescued or else the world will come to an end. You don't know me, but from reading, I know your brother and you too. Someone sent me your book from Warsaw. I told myself that something must be done. What's the sense in sleeping? A bear sleeps all winter and he remains a bear. So that was how I got the opportunity to meet your brother in person and now you as well. I simply telephoned the big shots at the border. America isn't Russia. Here when you phone, you get information. Our greenhorns are afraid to call an office, but a telephone doesn't bite. Here in America, I've already spoken to governors, senators. Such calls cost money, but money was made to spend, not be kept under a pillow. What I'm getting at is, now that you're back in America and a free man, thank God, a celebration is in order. There is a restaurant here with a roof garden. That's America for you. They plant a garden on a roof and the garden is a restaurant offering the finest food, entertainment. Our fathers and grandfathers wouldn't have eaten there, but as far as I know, none of you is that pious. I propose that you accompany me there as my guests. It would be a great honor and a pleasure as well for me—"

The whole time Reuben Mecheles was talking, my brother was casting questioning glances at me and at

Zosia. From time to time, he nodded to Reuben Mecheles. He said, "I thank you, Mr. Mecheles, but I'm having company tonight at home. Maybe some other time. I'll be glad to reimburse you for all the money you spent on the calls—"

"No, no, no! I'm not dunning you for any money. Simply to meet you is worth everything in the world to me. When do we, common people, have the privilege to be with writers, and with talented writers at that? I truly hope we will meet again. I have things to tell you that, when you heard them, they would stand your hair on end, that is, if you had hair. Not fabricated things but facts that I myself have witnessed and experienced, in my own case and with other people—some as good as angels and others vicious devils. Allow me to present you with my visiting card. I'm no writer, but from what I would tell you, you could write the greatest works. Do our writers know what goes on in the world? They sit in the Cafe Royal and gossip and this to them is the world. Promise me that you'll call!"

Reuben Mecheles seized my brother's hand in his small hands. My brother promised to phone him. He nodded to Zosia but he ignored me completely. He left and the three of us remained momentarily silent. Zosia had revealed the secret that she went with me to Toronto and my brother probably assumed that I had conducted this adventure on the money he had deposited in the bank in my name. Until I managed to withdraw the money from the bank and return it to him, he would consider me a swindler.

5

Neither Zosia nor I wanted to go to the roof-garden restaurant. Zosia explained that she wasn't properly dressed and that she wasn't hungry besides. She hadn't slept all night and she wanted to retire early. I had slept a few hours and I was hungry, but I didn't have the slightest urge for amusement and roof gardens. I proposed that we go instead to the Steward Cafeteria, but at the very word "cafeteria," Reuben Mecheles grimaced and said that it couldn't be otherwise but that I was trying to insult him. After a while, he proposed that we go up to his apartment on Riverside Drive. He didn't even wait for an answer. He took Zosia's arm and led her out into the corridor. I closed the door and followed them down the narrow stairs. It wasn't until I was downstairs that it struck me that I should have taken along my passport with the visa and the card. I had read in the *Forward* about thieves who specialized in stealing passports and other documents and using them to bring in illegal aliens. But I didn't want to detain Reuben Mecheles, who had lost sleep, time, and money on my account.

On Fourth Avenue he hailed a cab and we got in. Reuben Mecheles lit a cigar and said, "Since my wife has left me and I've reverted to being a bachelor, I've stopped eating at home. Still, you'll get a better meal at my house than you would in those cafeterias where you can ruin your stomach. I have a new refrigerator and everything is fresh. I'm usually not hungry during the day, but in the middle of the night a hunger comes over me and I always keep food ready. I have been an insomniac for many years. I wake up exactly at two o'clock every morning and rummage around like a sleepwalker. I take walks which are absolutely dangerous. I take taxis just to be able to see how New York looks in the early hours. I like to talk to the taxi drivers and to hear their strange stories. That's how God arranged it—that those who know life can't write, while those blessed with talent are dreamers who know only their own fantasies. Zosia has undoubtedly told you something about me, but she is an impractical person herself. I call her a yeshiva student in skirts. You won't believe this, but I knew her father when he was still the head of a yeshiva on Twarda Street, and also later when he turned his coat, as the saying goes. What he did is incomprehensible, but where is it written that we have to understand everything? A time has come when all people are searching for something. The Torah is certainly a great book and the prophets were divine men and even Jesus of Nazareth can't be lightly dismissed. But all this isn't enough for modern man. There is a hunger for something more. What is Stalin? And what is even such a murderer as Hitler? False prophets. Since no one has been in heaven and

God doesn't come down to the earth and remains silent from generation to generation, how can one know wherein lies the truth? I listen to everyone, even if he preaches that there is a horse fair on the moon."

"Oh, I forgot to ask you—what's new with your prophet? What's his name again? Is he still on Ellis Island?" Zosia asked.

"They've released him, but he got sick and he is in Lakewood recuperating," Reuben Mecheles replied after some hesitation. "Why do you call him *my* prophet? I didn't discover him and I don't consider him a prophet. He wrote a work that can't be considered anything else but religious. He speaks in the name of God, but in my estimation, this is nothing more than a means of expressing truths as one man sees them. The acknowledged prophets weren't in heaven and God didn't speak to them either. Someone in the Gemara says that Moses never rose higher than ten cubits from Mount Sinai. He sat there on a rock and carved out the Ten Commandments. Whether he fasted the forty days or not doesn't concern me. If this be the case, why can't someone of our generation do the same? In what way is a fountain pen worse than a chisel and hammer? I am, as you see, a realist—"

The taxi had pulled up before a tall building on Riverside Drive, just a few blocks from where my brother lived. But this was a fancier house, with a uniformed doorman, a richly furnished lobby, with oriental rugs, paintings, tropical plants. The elevator had an upholstered bench—something I was seeing for the first time. Reuben Mecheles' apartment looked like a museum. All the walls were covered with paintings almost to the carved ceilings. There were antiques everywhere. Old books peered out of glassed cabinets along with objects made of silver and ivory. There were spice boxes, crowns and fescues for Torah scrolls, Chanukah lamps, Passover platters.

Reuben Mecheles said, "I have every kind of luxury here outside of a maid. My wife—I can already call her my ex-wife—couldn't get along with any maid. She kicked up such a fuss about every trifle that the maids fled from her. Now a woman comes here twice a week but I've learned to fix my own meals. Come into the dining room and I'll be your waiter."

"I'll help you," Zosia proposed.

"No, I won't allow it. By me, a guest is a guest, especially such honored guests. Here in America, there are no aristocrats. Here, a millionaire rolls up his sleeves and washes his car. Here, things are easy. I phone and they send everything up. It's summer outside but inside my refrigerator it's winter. I'll bring you whatever I have and you'll choose what you like. My kitchen is like a grocery. I'll show it all to you later."

Reuben Mecheles went to the kitchen. Zosia asked, "Why did his wife leave him? She had a paradise here."

"Now it can be yours," I said.

"No, it's not for me. He has established for himself a

palace here, but he is always off to somewhere. He can't sit home a minute. He has told me things about himself that have revolted me. It's clear now that he went to Reno to plead with his shrew to come back to him. After what has happened between us, I'll never start up with anyone again."

I rose and began to study the paintings. Each picture was interesting individually, but collectively they exuded an air of tedium that astonished me. How could this be? Hundreds of talents had worked on these paintings and drawings. I felt often similar reactions in a library. I stood among the masterworks of world literature and yet I knew in advance that not one of those books could dissipate my misery. I actually felt better in my empty room. There, at least, no one tried to amuse me or to point the way to the truth.

Reuben Mecheles came in with a huge tray of food— bread, rolls, cake, milk, cream, cheese, sausage, fruit. He said, "If you're still hungry after all this, call me what my ex-wife called me—a phony."

6

Following the meal, Reuben Mecheles opened a drawer and handed me a huge mimeographed manuscript, so heavy that I could barely lift it. The title page proclaimed that this was the Third Testament, a Torah that God had revealed to the Prophet Moses ben

Ephraim. The manuscript contained both the Hebrew text and its English translation for a total of nearly two thousand pages.

We went into the living room and I began to leaf through the pages and scan a line here and there. The first chapters recorded that Moses ben Ephraim was a Sephardi, from his father's side a tenth-generation Sabra. His mother was from Jerusalem but her parents came from Egypt. The revelation had come to Moses ben Ephraim in a cave not far from Safad. He had run away from home to study the cabala with a blind cabalist. One night when the blind master had gone off to spend the night on Rachel's grave, the cave had grown brilliant as if from a thousand suns and Moses had heard a voice. . . .

I flipped through the pages at random—a scriptural style. The Almighty bade all the nations should become a single people and study the Torah of Moses ben Ephraim. God had revealed that Hitler was a descendant of Amelek and that the English who had come to America on the *Mayflower* were all descendants of the Lost Tribes of Israel. God had labeled Roosevelt "my messenger." He had praised Wilson and had predicted that following Hitler's defeat the League of Nations would shift to Mount Zion in the land of Israel and Moses ben Ephraim would use the League as an instrument by which to teach the nations justice and bring about peace and unity. All people would speak a common tongue—Hebrew. The children would also be taught Aramaic and English in the schools. Lord Balfour and Herzl would be among the saints who would be resurrected and belong to the Sanhedrin of seventy-one elders headed by Moses ben Ephraim.

I skimmed some hundred or so pages and learned that Jesus of Nazareth and his apostles had been true prophets. Judas Iscariot had not been a traitor but had remained loyal to Jesus. The tale of the thirty pieces of silver had been fabricated by idolators in Rome. In subsequent chapters, God revealed that Stalin was a product of Haman and Vashti, who had betrayed King Ahasuerus and had been a secret mistress of Haman's.

Reuben Mecheles said, "You're smiling, eh? The world needs a new creed. The concept of a chosen people has done the Jews lots of harm. You're only scanning the book but I took the trouble to read it from beginning to end. Mankind must be united, not torn apart into races and cliques. The first Moses was a person, not an angel. He ordered the murder of the Canaanites, the Hittites, and the Amorites, but Moses ben Ephraim calls all gentiles brothers. He wants peace between Isaac and Ishmael, between Jacob and Esau, between the whites and the Negroes. I don't believe in his miracles, but he wants unity, not a splintered humanity."

"I'm sorry to say that Moses ben Ephraim won't unite mankind," I said.

"Who then will unite it?"

"No one will."

"You mean to say that people will always hate each other and wage wars and that there will never be peace?"

"It's entirely possible."

"And you can come to terms with that notion?"

"Do I have a choice?"

"Well, I can't. I must believe that the human species is growing better, not worse."

"On what do you base your belief?"

"I don't know myself on what. After all, we were once apes and now we're humans. It's a long distance between a gorilla and Mahatma Gandhi or our Chafetz Chayim. You mustn't think that I don't know what goes on in the world. I've seen all kinds of villains—among Russians, among Poles, even among us Jews. I lived for years with the most wicked woman. No matter what I gave her it wasn't enough. No matter how good I was to her, she kept demanding more and more and cursed, and abused, and threatened suicide and even murder. She spent a fortune on doodads, clothes that she never had the opportunity to wear, jewelry that was stolen or robbed from her, fake art. When she fell into a rage, she tore, trampled, burned costly things, threw them in the garbage. She cheated on me with every brute she met and even had the gall to bring them to my house. They slept in my bed, wore my pajamas. When the time came when I could stand no more and wanted to put an end to it, she found lawyers as vicious as herself—Jewish lawyers—

and they took everything I had. The American courts of law, which are supposed to concern themselves with justice, promptly took her side because not the victims but the evildoers and the criminals support the lawyers and the judges.

"I saw all this and much more, but I still couldn't completely lose my faith in man or my hopes for a better world. My mother, may she rest in peace, didn't behave like my wife. She bore my father eleven children and she buried seven out of the eleven. She worked at home and in the store sixteen hours a day, if not more, while Father sat in the study house or went to his rabbi's where he dallied for weeks on end. As poor as we were, Father, may he rest in peace, brought a pauper for dinner on the Sabbath and Mother took the food out of her own children's mouths to carry food to the poorhouse. . . ."

It grew silent for a while. Reuben Mecheles took a handkerchief from his pocket and wiped the sweat off his brow.

Zosia said, "May I ask you something? If you can't answer me, it doesn't matter."

"What do you want to ask?"

"How was it you flew to Reno to make up with such a wife?"

Something akin to a tearful smile came over Reuben Mecheles' face. "I'm crazy, that's what I am. I once read of a professor who predicted that all mankind would come to an end because of madness. Everyone would go berserk. It's not far from this now. If Russia lets itself be ruled by a maniac like Stalin, and Germany by a Hitler, how far is it from the time when the whole world will turn mad? My madness consists of the fact that I was cursed with an overdose of compassion. I try to put myself in another's place, to learn what led him or her to do what they did. There is a book out by a professor who maintains that criminals are not responsible for their acts. If a murderer kills someone the killer should be taken to a sanitarium and kept there until he is cured. Naturally, the cost for this would be borne by those who work to support themselves and their families. The truth is that the human species is already crazy and I am a part of it."

I had an urge to ask Reuben Mecheles how he could afford to pay rent for such a large apartment and how he had managed to accumulate so many paintings and antiques when his wife took everything away from him, but I decided against it.

Zosia said, "It's late. I must go."

"Where are you staying? Back in the same hotel?"

"Yes, there."

"You can sleep here if you like. I mean the both of you. I have not one bedroom but three, and I'm not going to spy on you through the keyhole."

"I thank you, but I must go," Zosia replied.

"I hope you'll be staying in New York for a while yet," Reuben Mecheles said.

"No, I'm going back to Boston tomorrow."

CHAPTER TEN

I

That summer was a hot one. The air in New York was stifling. My brother had invited me repeatedly to come stay with him at the seashore, but I remained in the city. In my mind, Seagate was connected with Nesha and Nesha had married that would-be writer and genuine fellow traveler Zachariah Kammermacher, whom I had encountered in Paris and later in her house that evening when I had been delayed in coming to see her.

I had had a long chat with her on the phone. Nesha had told me that she didn't love Zachariah and she knew that she never would, but she lacked the strength to go on working. She had reached a stage in which she had been seriously considering suicide. She hadn't deceived him. She had told him frankly that she couldn't love him, but Zachariah Kammermacher had told her that he didn't believe in love. He had been widowed and he needed someone to run his household. He had a married daughter and a son who had been educated in England. The Communists provided Zachariah with all kinds of ways to earn money—articles in their magazines, lectures. He had a job on their Yiddish newspaper. He had a spacious apartment on West End Avenue and a summer house near Poughkeepsie. He had offered to adopt Nesha's son. Nesha said the usual things women say in such instances: She would never forget me, we would remain friends. At the same time, she hinted that she was sick and that she didn't expect to live much longer. I asked her the nature of her illness and she replied, "Everything."

Two years passed by but I had been left alone. I heard nothing more from Stefa or from Lena. Only my cousin wrote to me. She had married an electrician from Galicia. Her friend, Tsipele, had gone to live with her uncle who had left his wife. I had read in a Yiddish newspaper that "the well-known philanthropist and art collector Reuben Mecheles had married Miss Zosia Fishelsohn," a convert to Christianity who reconverted to Judaism, and the pair went to live in Jerusalem.

My state of mind had robbed me of the appetite to write to such an extent that I had to make an effort each week to complete my brief column, "It's Worthwhile Knowing." My fountain pen invariably leaked and made blots. My hand cramped. My eyes took part in the sabotage, too. I had heard of hay fever while still in Poland, but I had never suffered from it there. All of a sudden, I started sneezing in August of that year. My nose became stuffed up, my throat grew scratchy, my ears filled with water and developed a ringing and a whistling. I took a daily bath and kept myself clean, but I suffered from an itch and had constantly to scratch. No pills helped my constipation. I spent whole days in bed being baked by the sun that shone in through my window from noon to twilight. I didn't even bother to lower the shade. My sexual fantasies grew even more bizarre. By day I dozed, at night I stayed awake. I still brooded on the mysteries of the universe. Maybe it was possible to find a way to penetrate the enigmas of time and space, the categories of pure reason, the secret of life and consciousness? I had read somewhere that Einstein had for years been searching for a kind of super-Newtonian formula that would include gravity, magnetism, and the electromagnetic forces. Maybe there existed somewhere a formula that could combine—along with what Einstein was seeking— life, thought, and emotion as well? Maybe there existed such a combination of words and numbers that would encompass the whole riddle of Creation?

Neither God nor nature could hide forever. Sooner or later must come the revelation. Maybe it was I who was destined to receive it. I mentally tabulated everything that I had read of the philosophers, the mystics, the modern physicists. Einstein was right, I told myself, God didn't play dice. Somewhere there was a truth that explained Chmielnitzki's outrages, Hitler's madness, Stalin's megalomania, the exaltation of a Baal Shem, every vibration of light, every tremor of the nerves. There were nights when I awoke with the feeling that I saw the formula in my dream, or at least some part of it and I stayed awake for hours trying to recollect what I saw.

Each week when I delivered my column late at night I groped in the mail box, but no one wrote to me. I had broken away from people and they had abandoned me. An indolence settled over me. I even lacked the energy to eat at the cafeteria and I missed meals. I had fallen into a crisis that could last to the end of my life.

One day in mid-July, someone knocked on my door. I opened it and saw a man and a young woman. Both their faces seemed familiar but I had forgotten their names as well as where and when I had met them. I stood there for a moment looking at them, perplexed. The man said, "I swear he doesn't recognize me. It's me, Zygmunt Salkin."

"Oh, yes, yes, yes! Come in! Welcome!"

"We met on your first day in America. This young lady is Anita Komarov. She tells me that she gave you your first English lesson."

"Yes, I remember! What a pleasant surprise. Such guests!"

I wanted to extend my hand to my visitors but my palm was wet. I was wet all over. Anita said, "What a heat in here! Like a steel plant in Pittsburgh."

"Please, sit down."

As I said these words, it struck me that I had only one chair in my room and it was broken and strewn with papers, shirts, socks, underwear. The bed was unmade and the sheet showed traces of bedbugs. Across the cracked linoleum lay newspapers, magazines, and books I had taken out of the public library along with those I had bought on Fourth Avenue for a nickel each. Both Salkin and Anita had changed. Salkin's hair had grayed around the temples. He wore a light suit and white shoes. Anita was the daughter of a Yiddish poet, Zalman Komarov. Anita had attended a drama school. I had made her acquaintance when still in Seagate. She was petite, thin to the point of emaciation, with black hair that she kept as short as a boy's. She had a pointed Adam's apple also like a boy's. Her face was narrow, her cheeks sunken, her nose snub. She suffered from acne.

I heard Zygmunt Salkin say, "We didn't come here to sit. I've been looking for you for weeks. Where have you been hiding? Anita and I had a talk and it turned out that she knows you. We decided to find you at any price and here you are. Such heat as is in this room is rare even in Africa."

"I'm not shaved, and besides—"

"Come, come. You can melt here, and then it'll be too late. You may be aware that I've founded a group for young actors, and for old ones as well, if they have the talent. Something has to be done for the theater in America. There was a time when I dreamed about reviving the Yiddish theater, but I've convinced myself that this was a waste of time. If something can be done for the English theater, this may help the theater in other languages. The theater is like a body. If you help one part, it influences the other parts. Besides, this gives me an opportunity to meet young and pretty girls. Isn't that so, Anita?"

Zygmunt Salkin smiled and winked, and Anita winked back and said, "All men, without exception, are egotists."

Anita had told me her life story. At the age of seventeen, she had been involved in an affair with a Morris Katzenstein, a philosophy student at City College, son of the Yiddish actor Shamai Katzenstein. Anita (her parents called her Hannele) moved in with Morris and became pregnant. The parents on both sides demanded that the couple marry and they arranged a quick wedding, but during the honeymoon in Bermuda, Anita miscarried. Morris later became a Communist and gave up his studies. He also left Anita and went to live with a female activist among the Reds who was ten years older than he. Anita, an only daughter, moved back in with her parents. I had met her at Nesha's house.

I had forgotten that Salkin had his own car; it was now parked outside of the decrepit building in which I lived. Actually, it was the same car in which he picked me up the day I arrived in America. My brother told me that Salkin lived with a mistress in the area called Greenwich Village.

I had assumed that he would take Anita and me to a restaurant, but he let me know that he was taking us to his place where there would be a party. Had he told me this sooner, I would have changed my suit and shaved as well. Now, he had presented me with a *fait accompli.*

I was far from in the mood for meeting strangers. I had an urge to tell Salkin sharply that I wasn't some kind of rare animal to be put on exhibit at will, and to demand that he leave me alone, yet at the same time I knew that Salkin was out to help me, not humiliate me. He seemed to be in a cheerful mood. He was humming some song and he joked with Anita. He had turned into Fifth Avenue and he pointed out to me buildings, a hotel, a restaurant—all of which were connected with famous American writers or painters of whom I had never heard.

Soon we entered the narrow streets of Greenwich Village. Both the men here and the women appeared to me half naked. I saw youths with beards and long hair, in sandals on bare feet, in yellow, green, red trousers. One smoked a long pipe, another carried a monkey in a cage, a third had a placard draped over his back and as he walked he drank some liquid from a bottle and shouted slogans. The women displayed their independence in their own fashion. One walked about barefoot, a second led a huge dog on a leash and pushed a carriage containing a Siamese cat, a third wore a straw hat the size of an umbrella. Artists exhibited paintings on the narrow sidewalks. A poet sold his mimeographed poems. The neighborhood reminded me of Paris and of Purim.

The car stopped before a house with a dark, narrow entrance. We climbed up four flights and Salkin opened a door into a large, dim room filled with men and women. Apparently the party had already started. On a long table covered with a red tablecloth red candles burned in holders. It smelled here of whiskey, wine, meat, perspiration and of the lotions women use to subdue the odors of the flesh. The people were all talking, laughing, expressing interest in some bit of news that seemed to raise everyone's spirits. Out of the crowd pushed Salkin's mistress—blond, blue-eyed, wearing a white blouse and a long skirt embroidered in gold and silver. Her red fingernails were long and pointed. A cigarette in a long holder extended from between her red lips. On one of her fingers was a ring resembling a spider. Salkin introduced her as Lotte. For a moment she appeared to be young, a girl of perhaps eighteen or nineteen, but then I saw the wrinkles at the corners of her eyes and the slackness in her neck that no makeup could hide. When Salkin announced my name and added whose brother I was, over her face came that sweet smile and glow of confidence that worldly women can evoke at any time and under any circumstance. She tried to speak to me in Yiddish and soon switched over into English: "Your brother talks of you whenever we meet. Salkin, too. He's read your book—what's its name?—and he was enchanted. Unfortunately, I can't read Yiddish, but my grandmother used to read the Yiddish newspaper every day. Zygmunt tells me that you hide from everyone. But today he vowed that he would nab you. What are you drinking?"

"Oh, nothing. Maybe some soda."

"That's all? At a party you have to drink. Wait a minute, the phone is ringing."

How odd, but I had forgotten all about my bash-

Raphael
Soyer

fulness. It was almost dark in here and no one would be able to tell whether my suit was pressed or wrinkled, whether I was shaved or not. After a while, Salkin and Anita drifted away and I was left alone. I walked over to a table on which bottles of liquor were standing. I noticed that the guests poured drinks for themselves. I knew what I had to do—get drunk. I picked up one of the bottles and poured myself a half glassful. It was cognac. I took one large gulp and drained the glass. A burning blazed up in my throat and soon after in my stomach. A bowl of rolls stood on the table and I quickly bit into one. I felt the fumes of the alcohol rushing to my brain. My head began to spin and my legs wobbled. Since everyone was drinking, I mused, they probably weren't so sure of themselves either. Apparently, they too suffered from inferiority complexes. I wasn't drunk, nor was I sober. I poured myself a little more of the liquor. I noted that the guests were walking around with the drinks in their hands and I did the same. A black maid carrying a tray came up and spoke to me but I didn't hear what it was. After a while, I caught on that she was offering me something to eat from the tray. I wanted to pick up a half of hard-boiled egg with a toothpick, but it slipped from my hand. Instead, I took something with cheese. The maid handed me a red paper napkin. She smiled at me, showing a mouthful of white teeth. I pushed my way through the crowd of strangers. Someone trod on my foot, excused himself, apparently made a

241

joke, since he himself laughed at what he had said. Salkin came up and soon Anita joined us. Salkin said, "Let's go into the bedroom. There's something I want to discuss with you."

The bedroom had a bed so wide that not one couple but two or even three could have slept in it comfortably. A painting of some red smudges hung here and a lithograph of people standing on their heads, flying through the air. There was a figure of a man with horns and the snout of a pig, and of a female with breasts in front and behind, all apparently painted by the same artist. Salkin and Anita sat down on the bed and I settled in a wicker chair. Salkin said, "We, Anita and I, have a plan to propose to you, but before you say no, hear me out first. I've already told you about our theater troupe. We leased a place in the Catskills in which to rehearse and talk over all our problems. None of us gets a penny. On the contrary, we contribute to the effort. We plan—not this year but a year from now—to put on a play that will infuse new life into the theater. What we have there is not a theater but a hotel casino. The hotel itself burned down, or the owner set it on fire. The casino was far removed from the hotel and it remained in one piece. There is a small stage there and benches and that's all we need. Anita's parents live not far away. It was actually through her that I learned about this casino. There is a Yiddishist summer colony nearby, with bungalows named after Yiddish writers and Socialist leaders—

Peretz, Sholem Aleichem, Mendele, Bovshover. Anarchists stay there too, that is to say, ex-anarchists who are now businessmen, some of them even millionaires, and have bungalows with names like Rosa Luxemburg, Peter Kropotkin, Emma Goldman. Some of these ex-revolutionaries help our group with small donations. It would pay you to see the whole setup. You would have something to write about. I spoke with your brother about you and he is irked because you have isolated yourself from everything and everybody. This may be good for an elderly writer whose career is over, D'Annunzio or Knut Hamsum, not for a young man. I normally wouldn't take a place in the Catskills for the summer, but since I am the founder of the group and basically responsible for everything that happens there, we, my friend Lotte and I, rented a house in that area and we'll be spending the rest of the summer there, at least until Labor Day. We have a lot of rooms in this house, more than we can use, and we would like for you to come stay with us. First of all, you'll save the rent you're paying. Second, you'll get some fresh air, not sit, if you'll excuse me, in a stinkhole. Third, you can help us."

"How?"

"We've been a long time searching for a suitable play for an experimental theater and it occurred to me that Peretz's *At Night in the Old Marketplace* wouldn't be a bad idea. You undoubtedly know the thing. It's not for the general audience. As often as it has been staged, it has inevitably been a flop—in Poland and here, too. It's a play full of symbolism and mysticism. That's the very reason it would be good for us. I've translated the thing into English and I've read it to the group and although three quarters of them aren't Jewish—American young men and girls from Texas, Missouri, and Ohio, and what have you—they understood the play and were enraptured by it. The play could draw a number of the native-born Jews who are interested in Yiddish art—but only if it is done in English, not in Yiddish. The play, as you know, has a lot to do with the cabala and Jewish mysticism, and those are unfamiliar areas for me. I want to direct the play and you could be of great help to me.

"I want to tell you something else. I read your *Satan in Goray* and I have a high opinion of it. I told this to your brother and he fully agrees with me. If *At Night in the Old Marketplace* should turn out a success—I mean an artistic success not a financial one—sooner or later we would be able to dramatize your work and I could even get you an advance of a few hundred dollars. In brief, Anita, Lotte, and I want to drag you out of the rut into which you've fallen or thrown yourself. And I ask you— don't be too quick to say no. Our group has no money, no experience, and no name, but all things start out small. Where Times Square is now was a farm where goats grazed a hundred years ago. Isn't that so, Anita?"

"If not a hundred years ago, then a hundred and fifty years ago."

"What's your answer?"

"I'm not sure that I can help you."

"I'm sure that you can. Simply to discuss with you the various attitudes would be helpful to us. You'll be able to go on writing your articles. There is a library not far from us and a store where you can get the magazines from which you gather your so-called facts."

"Is there a cafeteria there?"

"What do you need with a cafeteria? Lotte is a woman with a lot of education and she's a talented actress besides, but she's also a splendid cook. She'll prepare your vegetarian dishes for you. We have other girls to cook as well. We live there actually in a kind of commune. Each person contributes whatever he or she can. Several of the girls come from wealthy homes. Your brother has promised to come stay with us for a few days."

"My mother and father would like to meet you, too," Anita said. "Normally they are busy all year but they take time out for vacations. We actually live there in that Yiddishist colony. Ours is the David Frishman bungalow. We are sunk in Yiddishism up to here—"

And Anita pointed to her chin.

2

From extreme isolation I was transported into extreme sociability. On one side was the theater group under the leadership of Zygmunt Salkin, and on the other the Yiddish poet Zalman Komarov, his wife, Bessie, and the colony of Yiddishists. I couldn't believe that such an abrupt transformation was possible. Zygmunt Salkin gave me the English translation of *At Night in the Old Marketplace* as well as the Yiddish text. I found many errors in the translation and Salkin promptly corrected them.

Even before, I had known that this play was too lacking in dramatic action to interest a theater audience and I proposed that it be played in conjunction with a dramatized short story of Peretz's. Salkin and his group seized upon this notion and they decided as one that I should be the one to choose the right story and to dramatize it in collaboration with Salkin.

When Zalman Komarov and the other Yiddishists heard that I was getting ready to dramatize something by Peretz—the spiritual leader and founder of Yiddishism —I became an overnight target of their interest. Yiddishism in America suffered a lack of young forces. I was comparatively young and my book had already received some notice among the Yiddishists even though the critics complained that I failed to follow in the path of the Yiddish classicists and gave myself over excessively to sex, as well as demonstrating a lack of concern with social problems.

I was now surrounded by people all day and sometimes half the night. Bessie Komarov, Anita's mother, often invited me for lunch, for dinner, sometimes even for breakfast. Lotte cooked my vegetarian meals. The group had many more women than men. Everyone was young and full of amateurish enthusiasm; I was to them an expert in Jewishness, which already at that time had begun to make inroads into American literature and theater.

Zygmunt Salkin and Anita Komarov took every opportunity to speak of my talent and to predict that I would do great things in the future. I often told myself at that time that I should be overjoyed. In the rare times when I was left alone, I posed the same question to myself: Are you happy now or at least satisfied? But the answer was always—no.

At that time I hardly ever read a newspaper, but Zygmunt Salkin received Yiddish newspapers from America, Poland, France, and even Russia, and a day didn't go by that I didn't learn of the deaths and all kinds of tragedies suffered by people who had been known or been close to me, or whom I knew through reading. And what about those whom I didn't know? What about the thousands, hundreds of thousands, actually millions of victims of Stalin's terror, Hitler's murders? What about the innocent people who had perished in Spain, in Ethiopia, in Mongolia, and who knows where else? What about the millions who suffered from cancer, consumption, or who starved to death? Even in America gangs of criminals killed and tortured their victims while phony liberals, cunning lawyers, and callous judges tolerated it all and actually helped the criminals with all sorts of pretexts and senseless theories. One would have to be totally indifferent toward man and beast to be able to be happy.

The Yiddishist colony seethed with those offering ready-made remedies for all the world's ills. Some still preached anarchism—others, socialism. Some placed all their hopes in Freud while others hinted that Stalin was hardly as bad as the capitalist lackeys painted him. Surely, no one in the colony considered the evils perpetrated daily upon God's creatures by the millions of hunters, vivisectionists, and butchers.

I had gained companionship, but my isolation from everything and everybody remained the same. All that was left were means of temporary forgetfulness. In order to get myself through the days and nights, I had to somehow muffle my senses. There were days when it seemed that Anita might provide this opportunity to me. However, something was holding us back—no moral inhibition but, one might say, a chemical one. In the course of my life I had often encountered these inhibitions. Although both sides were ready, some force that is stronger than their resolves said no. There were in the group girls who would gladly have had an affair with me, but despite my eagerness, the male within me demanded devotion and old-fashioned love.

For a while it appeared that our plan to put on *At Night in the Old Marketplace* was on its way. Zygmunt Salkin had gotten promises from alleged theater patrons that they would support the project with cash contributions. There was talk of leasing a theater in New York, if not on Broadway, then off-Broadway. But I was less deceived by these hopes than the others. Most of the boys and girls in the group had been left penniless. Zygmunt Salkin was actually the only patron of the organization and he was far from wealthy. To rent a theater required a contract and a deposit. The play needed scenery, the actors and actresses had to get enough to at least pay their rent and eat. At the rehearsals, I saw that Zygmunt Salkin lacked the skills of a director and that most of the boys and girls had little talent. Peretz's words emerged false, awkward, and often ridiculous from their mouths.

The month of August was almost over, and Labor Day —which signifies the end of many summer affairs, dreams, promises, and projects—was fast approaching. The Yiddishist colony began slowly to empty out. A number of those who in the heat of summer had preached socialism, the dictatorship of the proletariat, anarchism, atheism, even free love, went back to New York for the Days of Awe along with their elderly wives. They all offered excuses for observing the holidays. Nearly all of them had religious relatives whose feelings they didn't want to hurt.

The bungalows of Karl Marx, Rosa Luxemburg, Peter Kropotkin, and Emma Goldman closed one after the other. Zygmunt Salkin assured the members of the group that he and Lotte would go on working for the "new theater." He had a briefcase full of papers and a head full of ideas and hopes, but deep inside we knew that it was all over.

I had heard some shocking news. Several of the girls in the group had gotten pregnant and would have to get abortions. At that time, this was no easy matter. It cost a lot (five hundred dollars was a fortune) and it also represented a danger. The young men appeared even guiltier than the girls.

The days had become cooler and shorter. The leaves on the trees began to yellow and I saw birds flying in flocks—probably on their way to warmer climates. The nights were colder and longer. I could not sleep and I went outside for a breath of fresh air. There was no more light coming from the bungalows and the sky was full of stars. God, or whoever He is, was still there, observing His Creation. A new theater? A new man? The old idolatry was here again. The stone and clay idols had been exchanged for a Gertrude Stein, a Picasso, a Bernard Shaw, an Ezra Pound. Everybody worshiped culture and progress. I myself had tried to become a priest of this idolatry, although I was aware of its falsehood. At its best, art could be nothing more than a means of forgetting the human disaster for a while. I walked over to the colony. It was silent as a cemetery. Most of those whose names the bungalows bore had departed this world, with its illusions, forever. Those who worshiped them would follow soon. I lifted up my eyes to the starry sky again and again as if in hope that some revelation might descend upon me from above. I inhaled the cold air and shivered.

One day I got into Zygmunt Salkin's car and he took me back to New York with Lotte. They must have quarreled, because both were silent. They did not even look at one another. After traveling for two hours or so, we stopped at a cafeteria for a cup of coffee and a piece of cake, and here Lotte and Salkin got into an argument in my presence. Lotte called Salkin a "phony." She complained, as so many worldly women do, that because of him she had wasted her "best years."

3

I had surrendered myself to melancholy and it had taken me prisoner. I did what it demanded—squandered my time on empty musings; on mental probes that could bring no benefit to me or to others; on searches for something I had never lost. I had presented creation with an ultimatum: Tell me your secret or let me perish. I stayed up nights and dozed by day. I knew full well that I should have called my brother but I had lost his phone number— an excuse for me to avoid seeing him and having to justify my lazy existence. It was quite possible that the editorial office wanted to tell me to stop sending in the weekly article, or maybe they had more work for me, but I hid from them in any case. As long as they kept sending me the check, I kept cashing it. I paid the five dollars rent

and spent the rest on meals at the cafeteria. When the
checks stopped coming, I could always commit suicide.
Death had become a familiar thing for me. In my room I
stepped on vermin. One moment there was a cockroach
—winged, with eyes, a sense of hearing, a stomach, a
fear of death, an urge to procreate. All of a sudden I
squashed it with my heel and it was nothing, or perhaps
turned back to the infinite sea of life which fashions a
man from a cockroach and from a cockroach, a man.

On my long walks through New York, I passed fish
stores and butcher shops. The huge fish that yesterday
was swimming in the Atlantic now lay stretched out on
ice with a bloody mouth and blank eyes, fare for millions
of microbes and for a glutton to stuff his potbelly with.
Trucks stopped before the butcher shops and men came
out carrying heads, legs, hearts, kidneys. How frivolously
the Creator squandered His powers! With what
indifference He disposed of His masterworks into the
garbage! He wasn't concerned with either my faith or my
heresy, my praises or my blasphemies. Someone had
warned me not to drink from the tap in my sink since this
could give me all kinds of sickness, but I burned with
thirst in the nights and I gulped from the rusted sink
till my abdomen grew as taut as a drum. I bought half-
rotted fruit in the street and stuffed myself on it, worms
and all. I stopped shaving daily and went about with a
stubble, with scuffed shoes and a stained suit. Like other
bums, I picked up newspapers and magazines in the gar-

bage cans. The scientists kept on discovering new particles in the atom, which was becoming more and more of a complicated system, a cosmos in itself, full of riddles that were to be solved in the future. More evidence came out that the universe is running away from itself, a result of an explosion that took place some twenty billion years ago. Substance and energy swap roles. Causality and purpose appear more and more like two masks of the same paradox. In Soviet Russia countless traitors and enemies of the people were purged and liquidated, among them Yiddish poets who had published long odes to Comrade Stalin. According to the reviews in the book sections of the newspapers and journals I read, new and remarkable talents emerged each month, each week, each day in a deluge of genius in the United States and all over the world. Small and isolated as the Yiddishist coterie was, it raved and ranted about its achievements in literature, in the theater, and mainly in helping to bring about the redemption of the peasants and workers everywhere. There was nothing I could do but stew in my own gloom. Like the universe, I had to run away from myself. But how? And where? When I was a cheder boy I once did a thing which I always regretted. I caught a fly, put it into a little bottle with a few drops of water and a crust of sugar, stopped it with a cork, and threw it into a cellar where the janitor of our building kept broken furniture, rags, useless brooms, and similar garbage. Why I committed this ruthless act I never knew. Now I have become this fly myself, doomed to expire in darkness, a victim of a power that played games with frail creatures. All I could do was cry out to the heavenly cheder boy, "Why did you do it? How would you feel if some supercelestial cheder boy would do the same to you?" I was beginning to ponder a religion of rebellion against God's indifference and the cruelty of those whom He created in His image.

The Chasidic rabbis whose books I once studied used to write down rules of conduct for themselves, as well as for others, on slips of paper which they called *tsetl koton* and I did the same, often in rhyme, so that they would be easy for me to remember. I fantasized about building temples of protest, study houses where people would contemplate and reminisce about the various misfortunes God has sent to humans and animals. The Book of Job would become their Torah minus God's answer to Job and the happy ending. I dreamed of a humanism and ethics the basis of which would be a refusal to justify all the evils the Almighty has sent upon us in the past and which He is preparing to bestow upon us in the future. I even played with the idea of nominating a new group of protesting prophets or saints, such as Job, Schopenhauer, Baudelaire, Edgar Allan Poe, Von Hartmann, Otto Weininger, Bashkirtsev, and some others who rejected life and considered death the only messiah. I remember calling those who flatter God and kiss the rod with which He smites them "religious masochists."

4

Outside, the autumn rain poured. Inside the office buildings on Nineteenth Street the lights were on all day long. The headlights of the passing trucks glared in the fog. I was too lazy to go out so I ate a combination of breakfast and lunch of stale bread and half-rotten bananas. On that evening I put on my shabby overcoat and went to Steward's Cafeteria on Twenty-third Street. I had paid my rent for the week and I was left with a dollar and forty-five cents. The cafeteria was half empty. I bought at the buffet a vegetable plate, a cup of coffee, and a dish of stewed prunes. Looking for a table where somebody had left a newspaper I found more than I expected: the New York *Times* and the *Daily Mirror*. I ate and fantasized. I was taking revenge for Dachau and Zbonshin. I gave back Sudetenland to the Czechs. I founded a Jewish state in Jerusalem. Since I was the ruler of the world, I forbade forever the eating of meat and fish and made hunting illegal. I was so busy bringing order to the earth that I let my coffee get cold. I counted my change and decided to spend another nickel for a second cup of coffee. On the way back with my coffee, I discovered the Sunday *Forward* on another table. Because the typesetters made so many mistakes in my column, "It's Worthwhile Knowing," I was not in a rush to turn to the page on which it usually appeared. Instead, I read the Jewish news. Even though the Communists in America denied it vehemently, it was clear that Stalin had liquidated not only a number of generals and such leaders as Bukharin, Zinoviev, Kamenev, and Rikov in his purges, but scores of Yiddish writers as well. A correspondent who had just returned from the Soviet Union reported that the number of victims of Stalin's purges had reached eight million. Hundreds of thousands of kulaks had died in their exile in Siberia. The "enemies of the people" were sentenced in mass trials. A lot of Communists who had come to the Soviet Union to help build Socialism were sent to work in the gold mines in the North, where the strongest man could not endure longer than a year.

I was drinking and shaking my head over the news. How could Jewish novelists, poets, and party leaders, grandchildren of our pious ancestors, defend such evil?

I was now ready to face the mistakes in my column. I found the page, but my column wasn't there. Instead, there was a long recipe for meat *kreplach*. They had stopped my column!

The cafeteria had emptied out. The lights were switched off and on to signal closing time. I paid my check to the cashier and returned to Nineteenth Street. It was still raining and in the four blocks between Twenty-third and Nineteenth streets I got drenched. I walked up the four flights to my room. It was too cold for the cockroaches to come out from their holes in the linoleum. There was no choice but to undress and go to bed. The blanket was thin and I had to put my feet into the sleeves of a sweater to warm them. I had turned out the ceiling light and was lying still. I fell asleep and dreamed. In the middle of the night someone knocked at my door. Who could it be? I had been told that Nazis lived in this building and I was afraid that someone might want to kill me. I looked around for something with which to defend myself. There was nothing except two wire clothes hangers.

"Who is it?" I asked.

"It's the night man."

The night man? What would a night man want in the middle of the night? I wondered. Aloud, I said, "What's wrong?"

"There is a cable for you."

"A cable? For me? So late?"

"The super gave it to me to give to you, but I forgot."

I rolled out of bed naked and fell to the floor. I got up, stripped the sheet off my bed and draped myself in it. Then I opened the door.

"Here."

And a black man handed me a cable.

I wanted to give him a nickel, but he didn't have the patience to wait and he slammed the door.

I tore open the cablegram and read:

Stuck in Athens with child. Send money at once.

Lena.

There was an address included that sounded Greek.

What kind of madness is this? I asked myself. Send money at once? This minute? What was she doing in Greece?

I threw off the sheet and glanced at my wristwatch. It had stopped at a quarter past five. Was it still today, or was it already tomorrow? It didn't matter either way. In Athens of all places . . . The rich uncle from America would send a check for $100,000, like in the trashy play at the Scala Theater. I felt like laughing, drinking the rusty water from the faucet and urinating. I stood for a while by the sink staring, as if seeking the means to fulfill all these three needs simultaneously. Then I went over to the window, opened it, and looked out into the wet street, its black windows, flat roofs, the glowing sky, without a moon, without stars, opaque and stagnant like some global cover. I leaned out as far as I could, deeply inhaled the fumes of the city, and proclaimed to myself and to the powers of the night:

I am lost in America, lost forever.

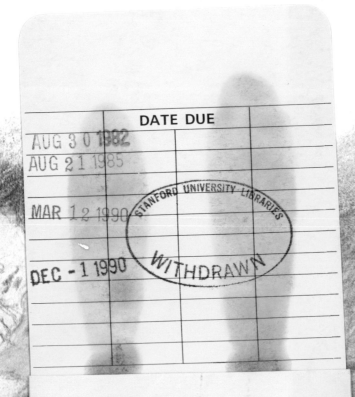